Inquiry Learning in the Gifted Classroom

Inquiry Learning in the Gifted Classroom takes readers step-by-step through the process of integrating, managing, and assessing problem-based learning (PrBL).

PrBL challenges students to think about problems in a logical manner, providing a structure for problem solving that can be used in any situation. Chapters begin with learning objectives and conclude with an activity designed to help readers master PrBL. Detailed, timely examples serve as guides that teachers can look to as they outline their own curriculum as well as helpful graphic organizers to aid in student assessment.

Built to foster lifelong learners, this book helps students experience firsthand how and what they learn in the classroom manifests and becomes relevant in their own lives. After all, it's a problem-based world out there.

Todd Stanley is the author of many teacher-education books including *Project-Based Learning for Gifted Students* (2nd edition), *Case Studies and Case-Based Learning, Using Rubrics for Performance-Based Assessment,* and *Authentic Learning: Real-World Experiences that Build 21st Century Skills*. He served as a classroom teacher for 18 years and is the gifted coordinator for Pickerington Schools. Follow him @the_gifted_guy or visit www.thegiftedguy.com.

Inquiry Learning in the Gifted Classroom

It's a Problem-Based World

Todd Stanley

Routledge
Taylor & Francis Group
NEW YORK AND LONDON

Cover image: © Getty Images

First published 2023
by Routledge
605 Third Avenue, New York, NY 10158

and by Routledge
4 Park Square, Milton Park, Abingdon, Oxon, OX14 4RN

Routledge is an imprint of the Taylor & Francis Group, an informa business

© 2023 Taylor & Francis

The right of Todd Stanley to be identified as author of this work has been asserted in accordance with sections 77 and 78 of the Copyright, Designs and Patents Act 1988.

All rights reserved. No part of this book may be reprinted or reproduced or utilised in any form or by any electronic, mechanical, or other means, now known or hereafter invented, including photocopying and recording, or in any information storage or retrieval system, without permission in writing from the publishers.

Trademark notice: Product or corporate names may be trademarks or registered trademarks, and are used only for identification and explanation without intent to infringe.

Library of Congress Cataloging-in-Publication Data
Names: Stanley, Todd, author.
Title: Inquiry learning in the gifted classroom: it's a problem-based world / Todd Stanley.
Description: New York: Routledge, 2023. | Includes bibliographical references. | Summary: "Inquiry Learning in the Gifted Classroom takes readers step-by-step through the process of integrating, managing, and assessing problem-based learning (PrBL). PrBL challenges students to think about problems in a logical manner, providing a structure for problem solving that can be used in any situation. Chapters begin with learning objectives and conclude with an activity designed to help readers master PrBL. Detailed, timely examples serve as guides that teachers can look to as they outline their own curriculum, and helpful graphic organizers aid in student assessment. Built to foster lifelong learners, this book helps students experience firsthand how and what they learn in the classroom manifests and becomes relevant in their own lives. After all, it's a problem-based world out there"– Provided by publisher.
Identifiers: LCCN 2022012352 (print) | LCCN 2022012353 (ebook) | ISBN 9781032299020 (Hardback) | ISBN 9781032299013 (Paperback) | ISBN 9781003302605 (eBook)
Subjects: LCSH: Problem-based learning. | Problem solving–Study and teaching. | Student-centered learning. | Gifted children–Education.
Classification: LCC LB1027.42 .S73 2023 (print) | LCC LB1027.42 (ebook) | DDC 371.95/69–dc23/eng/20220617
LC record available at https://lccn.loc.gov/2022012352
LC ebook record available at https://lccn.loc.gov/2022012353

ISBN: 978-1-032-29902-0 (hbk)
ISBN: 978-1-032-29901-3 (pbk)
ISBN: 978-1-003-30260-5 (ebk)

DOI: 10.4324/9781003302605

Typeset in Palatino
by Deanta Global Publishing Services, Chennai, India

This book is dedicated to Joel McIntosh and Katy McDowall.

Joel was the long-time heart and soul of Prufrock Press, starting it from scratch and providing a place where authors such as myself could have their voices heard when it comes to gifted education. Over the years, Joel has become more than my publisher, he has become a friend who is always looking out for me and including me in the conversation.

Katy was the editor for most of the books I wrote for Prufrock. It was always reassuring that when I handed over one of them to her, she was going to point out all of my stupid errors in a gentle manner and do her best to make it a better book. I always enjoyed getting to see her at conferences working the Prufrock table and I miss sending her emails when I have questions.

Contents

Introduction: It's a Problem-Based World   1

1   What is Problem-Based Learning?   6

2   What are the Benefits of Problem-Based Learning?   16

3   Steps to Problem-Based Learning   29

4   Finding Big Hairy Problems   39

5   Grading the Process   50

6   Keeping it Real: Authentic Learning   73

7   Raising the Rigor   85

8   The Power of Reflection   98

9   The Role of the Teacher   111

Conclusion: Houston, We Have a Problem   123

Appendix A: A PrBL for You   127
Appendix B: The Matrix   133
Works Cited   137

Introduction

It's a Problem-Based World

There are a lot of things we are taught in school that will never see the light of day in the real world. How many times have you had to use the periodic table in your day-to-day life? Has your boss ever once asked you to write a five-paragraph essay? How much of your understanding of the Northwest Ordinance has been of use in adulthood? And what the heck is Algebra II even for? There is a lot taught in school, and quite sadly, a lot forgot that was taught (whewww, say that five times really fast).

How do we decide what we should teach students then? If so much of what we learned is never to be used again, what could be taught that would be of some use to our own students? The mindset shift needs to be from "what" we teach, and rather focus on "how" we teach it. In the 21st century, content has become moot. We live in a day and age where information is at our fingertips, heck with some technology we don't even have to use our hands. And yet we are still asking students to memorize and know this information. However, Siri cannot change your flat tire. Alexa cannot cook dinner. No matter how many Google searches you do, you still have to wash your own clothes. You can watch a YouTube video on how to do your taxes but ultimately you are the one who has to do them. Each and every one of these situations is a problem. They might be minor problems, but they are problems nonetheless. And you need to figure out how to solve them, not because someone has assigned them to you, or because you are getting a grade for it. You have to learn how to solve them in order to be able to live your life.

DOI: 10.4324/9781003302605-1

It's a problem-based world and this is not just a catchy title to a book, it is reality. We are inundated with problems every…single…day. And there are two types of people when it comes to problem solving. Some people handle these problems quite well, learning how to adapt to a new situation, overcome an obstacle, or figure out another way. Others crumble when it comes to problems. When an obstacle is placed in their way, they simply stop in their tracks. Or they do not handle it in the most effective way and it balloons into an even greater problem.

What is the difference between these two groups of people, why are some folks able to come up with a great solution to the problem while others struggle? Like most things in life, the more we are exposed to something, the better we get at handling it. For example, when you are learning something simple such as how to multiply multi-digit numbers, students may find this very difficult at first because it is something they are not used to. You cannot just put the problem in front of the students and expect them to figure it out for themselves. But with teacher demonstrations and a number of practice problems, the students begin to see the logic behind the skill and become more comfortable with the concept. Once students gain an understanding of how it works, then they are able to multiple any multi-digit numbers. They have acquired that skill set.

This goes for larger, 21st-century skills as well. The more we have students participate in public speaking in our classes, the more at ease they become with it and the more likely that they are able to do this with some level of competency. They may be hesitant at first, but each time they have to give a public speech, they gain more and more confidence, and if they are provided with enough opportunities, they actually can become quite adept at it. Pretty soon they are able to give speeches in all sorts of situations because they have been exposed to it enough and developed that skill set.

The same goes for problem solving. The more we allow students to solve problems using a framework that supports this, the more comfortable they are going to be when something arises that takes problem-solving ability. Most people hear the term problem solving and immediately think of math. The kind of problem solving this book is referring to is taking on the big hairy problems. These are problems with many possible solutions, heck they can sometimes be problems that may not have any solution. Keep in mind though – it is not the solution where the learning is taking place. It is the process of trying to solve the problem, no matter what the outcome may be, where the greatest learning occurs. No problem is too big for this type of thinking. All things are considered.

How do you teach students how to do this though? The most important thing in teaching using problem-based learning (PrBL) is that students understand the structure they used so that it can be replicated in the future. By learning the how, it can be applied to any situation including ones in their own lives. This is going to take them much further in life than any knowledge about the periodic table or Northwest Ordinance or some other subject-specific information that they heard in school. This structure may be very obvious or it could be so subtle that you are not even aware it is there, but it is always there. This book will show you how you can set up this structure as well as creating a classroom culture that uses problem-based learning for student learning.

The book itself has a structure. Chapters 1 and 2 make the argument for the WHAT and WHY of PrBL. It is important that you buy-in to the importance of using such a learning strategy. If you don't believe in it, it will be very difficult to get your students to do the same. You want structure, we've got structure in Chapter 3, which shows the possibilities for how to present this to students. It starts with an overall structure that provides a roadmap and then provides details for what each of those steps can look like. Chapter 4 shows you how to look for what is called the big hairy problem. How does this problem relate to what you are supposed to teach, how does this problem connect to the lives of your students, and how can this problem lead to further exploration and learning, not just within the four walls of our school classroom, but in the interest and curiosity of learning.

In schools, we measure a lot of learning, usually in the form of right/wrong questions and standardized assessments. How do you grade something that may not have an answer? How do you measure what a student has learned when they cannot provide a solution? Again, this is a change in mindset. In PrBL, you should not be so focused on assessing the end result. The end result is just a by-product of what was learned during the process of gaining an understanding and figuring things out. This is the process of learning and is the most important aspect of a student's growth, but not something we assess very much. This is mostly because teachers do not know how to grade this process or how to grab something that seems intangible and make it measurable. It does take a different way of looking at things and a bit more effort, but you will know whether your students are truly learning or not. Chapter 5 shows you different ways in which you can measure what matters, which is the growth of your student as a learner.

School can something be a vacuum of learning where what is learned within the classroom stays in the classroom. This is because students cannot see the big picture of how it relates to their own lives, and more importantly, why they should care about what is being taught. There is a great scene about this in the movie *Peggy Sue Got Married* that starred Kathleen Turner. You can watch the clip by going here: www.youtube.com/watch?v=-3eKzmoz-vrI. In the clip, Peggy Sue has somehow traveled back in time from her life as a 45-year-old woman and landed back in high school. Her math teacher announces she has a test which Peggy then blows off by doodling all over the assessment. When the teacher asks what is the meaning of this, she calmly tells him that she will have no use for algebra in her life and she is speaking from experience. Although we do not have the luxury of traveling back in time to determine what we will and will not need to know in our lives, we do want to learn things that will have meaning to our lives and help us down the road not just in school, but in life. Too many times we are preparing our students for the next level of schooling when we should be preparing them for the next level of life. How do we do this? By having problems and assignments that are authentic, that are something the student would see outside of the classroom, and thus, would have use for. Chapter 6 teaches you how to keep it real and ensure that your problem, the product, and/or the audience is one that is authentic.

Chapter 7 shows you how such learning will raise the rigor in your classroom. This is a term we throw around a lot in education but not one we necessarily know how to do effectively. How do we make the learning more challenging so that we are having students thinking at the level of their potential? Especially gifted students who by definition have the most potential. We do this by giving them an assignment that has all sorts of possibilities and no ceiling. That is PrBL in a nutshell and it starts with the open-ended essential question.

One of the most powerful ways to ensure that the learning is going to stick is through the use of reflection. But it cannot be any old reflection, it needs to be purposeful and students need to be shown what effective reflection looks like. That is what Chapter 8 will show you how to do.

All of this may sound well and good, but I am sure you are thinking the thing you should be thinking about; what the hell does this look like in my classroom? Chapter 9 goes through what the role of the teacher may look like in such a learning environment and how this switches from being the purveyor of knowledge to creating a culture where students can become their own purveyors.

The book closes with a real-world, authentic example of problem-based learning at its finest, which is how do we get a person into space without killing them? This began with the space race in the 1960s and continues to this day as we try and explore beyond our own planet.

This book does contain two appendices, both designed to help you in the process of PrBL. The first one shows you a full-blown problem-based learning lesson that would be relevant to you as a teacher, which is creating a problem-based learning assignment that would be relevant to your students. Appendix B is a matrix that helps you to find problems, a product, an audience, and other aspects of PrBL. This can be used in your own planning.

Hopefully after the reading of this book, two things will occur:

1) You understand how to use PrBL in your classroom and see the benefit of doing so.
2) You feel comfortable in executing this learning strategy.

One thing that is for certain is if you are able to pull problem-based learning off in your classroom, your students will be the ultimate beneficiaries. How do you know this? Because you will be giving them the greatest gift a teacher can give to their student; something they can actually use in their own lives to make it better.

1

What is Problem-Based Learning?

> **Problem #1**
>
> *You have been tasked with giving a presentation on effective teaching strategies and have randomly been assigned problem-based learning as your strategy. Unfortunately, you have never used PrBL and so you need to learn more about it if you are going to be able to explain this to others.*
>
> *Your audience is a group of pre-service teachers who are just learning the trade and thus do not know a lot about teaching of any kind.*
>
> **Learning objectives:**
>
> ★ What is your understanding of problem-based learning?
> ★ How do you explain this to someone who knows nothing about it in such a way that makes them want to try it themselves?
> ★ How do you increase your own level of comfort to make you want to move forward in trying PrBL in your own classroom?

Problem-based learning is one of those terms in education that if you ask someone what it is, you might get several answers. This chapter will provide you with a clear definition of what PrBL is, and almost as important, what it is not. In addition to explaining what it is, this chapter will share with you what it looks like when using it in the classroom.

DOI: 10.4324/9781003302605-2

The umbrella of inquiry learning

Problem-based learning falls under the umbrella of inquiry learning. Inquiry learning is a classroom pedagogy where instead of the teacher presenting facts, there is a question, problem, or scenario presented for students to consider. Students then pose questions and research items in order to come up with a solution that expands their knowledge about the topic. What they are learning is found by them, not what the teacher has given them. It is discovery learning. It is also student-centered and active, meaning students will be engaged. In an inquiry classroom, the role of the teacher changes to more of a facilitator who guides the students, often with more questions that will expand the thought process rather than simple answers that will stifle it.

Several strategies are considered to be inquiry learning, problem-based being just one of those:

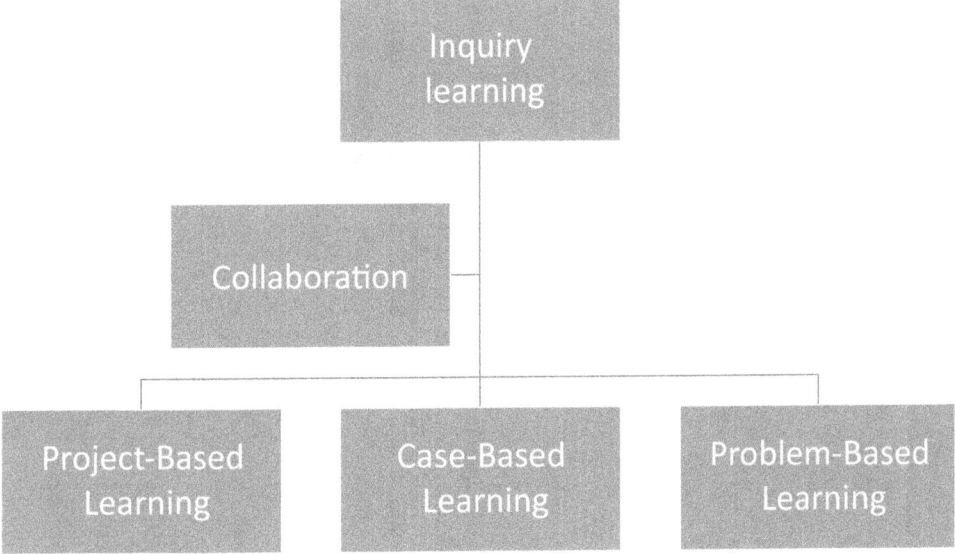

At the top is inquiry learning, which is at the heart of all of the other methods listed below. Inquiry learning begins with a question. This question can be posed by the students or provided by the teacher. Then it is up to the students to carry out the learning themselves, making decisions along the way and allowing the learning to take whatever shape they might make of it. Although there are slight differences in these strategies, the heart of the learning uses the inquiry learning process, which is as follows:

8 ◆ What is Problem-Based Learning?

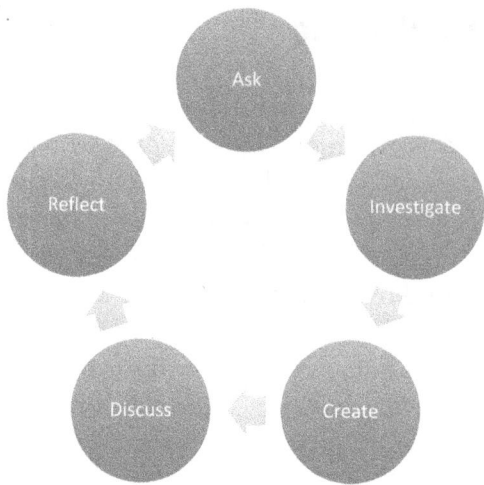

The description of each step is as follows:

Ask: using prior knowledge and understanding, have students pose an essential question or questions concerning a given topic.
Investigate: students then collect evidence to either prove or disprove the essential question.
Create: from this information, students are able to create a new understanding.
Discuss: students then present their findings, discussing and debating the results.
Reflect: the metacognition of thinking about what students learned from the activity.

This structure acts as the backbone for all of the other forms of inquiry learning.

Collaboration lies in between them because it brings more authenticity to learning when students collaborate in groups. The reason why collaboration is authentic is twofold:

1) By working in a group, students should be able to produce something better as a collective whole than they would individually. This describes about 95% of the workplaces where employees work together to achieve success. If anyone is not doing their part, the company can be affected as a result.
2) Collaboration is a valuable 21st-century skill that transcends the classroom and workplace. You will find yourself having to work with other people all of the time, whether it be family, friends, teammates,

and others. Knowing how to work together in a collaborative setting and being able to troubleshoot when problems arise is going to allow for a much easier time than for someone who has difficulties with others.

To make your problem-based learning more authentic, you should have students collaborating in groups as much as possible, using their collective energies to try and figure out a solution.

What's the difference?

The question becomes what distinguishes each of these three inquiry learning strategies from one another? The answer is what each of these focuses on, or what can be called the five Ps of authentic learning:

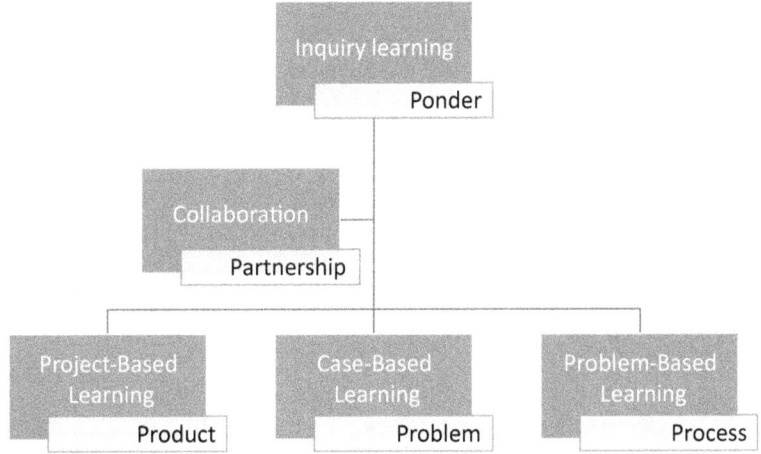

Project-based learning (PBL) focuses on the end. What is meant by this is that most PBL begins with the end *product* in mind and then works backward from there. For example, you want students to create a short story. You envision what this short story would look like when it is finished, then you determine what students need to learn to get to this point and you teach it to them or have them learn it themselves. When they put all of these skills together, what they have created is this end product that reflects the learning.

Case-based learning (CBL) on the other hand focuses on the beginning. What is the case or *problem* centered around from which all of the learning will stem from? It might be a primary document, a real-life situation, or an imagined one based on research and other information. All of the questions, learning objectives, and possible solutions come from this main source or sources that students get at the very beginning. For example, you decide to use the Supreme Court case of *Tinker v. Des Moines* to teach a unit on freedom of speech. Students can take a look at the case and determine what they need to learn about freedom of speech and where the line is drawn on what you can and cannot say in schools. They then might be able to connect it to their own school and the rules of policy of the Board of Education in regard to student voice. The case acts as the jumping-off point and gives you a base from which to have further discussion and learning.

Problem-based learning (PrBL) focuses not on the beginning or the end, but rather on what happens in between to branch these two together. It is the *process* where the learning is taking place. For example, your class decides to look at the problem of how to prevent birds from stealing kids' lunch boxes on the playground. Students may explore dozens of dead ends in trying to develop a viable solution but that is perfectly fine because what they are learning during this process is what does not work. They are also learning how to research, how to formulate learning objectives and questions, as well as how to determine a solution. It does not matter if this solution works or not. That is not the determining factor of success. It is the skills, content, and understanding gained while going through the process of trying to solve it.

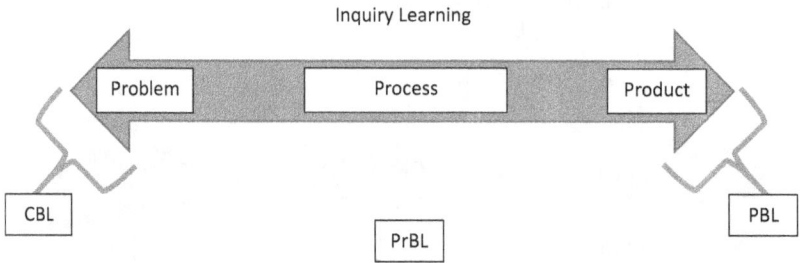

In addition to these three, you also have the overall structure of inquiry learning where you are challenging students to *ponder*. This requires a bit more than just questioning. Pondering means to think about something with more care, especially when trying to make a decision or reach a conclusion. It is unpacking all of the possibilities and exploring them, all the while learning. Collaboration involves a *partnership* where students combine abilities and skill-sets with the purpose of developing synergy to create something together.

Any one of these strategies is going to create a more authentic learning environment because it will be student-led, having them make most of the decisions themselves and guiding where to take the learning. And because the lesson is centered around an authentic situation, students are going to see how this applies to their own lives and thus see the relevance of it. This book is specifically going to be focused on problem-based learning. There will be some overlap with elements of project and case-based learning, but the examples and methods provided will be geared toward PrBL. If you would like to learn more about PBL or CBL, you can check out the following books that give a fairly extensive explanation of how to use these other strategies in the classroom:

Project-Based Learning for Gifted Students: A Step-By-Step Guide to PBL and Inquiry in the Classroom, 2nd edition (2020), Todd Stanley
Case-Studies and Case-Based Learning (2019), Todd Stanley

The difference between PrBL and the traditional classroom

What is the difference between was is termed a traditional classroom and this inquiry-based learning style of problem-based learning? There are lots of differences but there is one glaring one.

The process of problem-based learning

That difference is who is controlling the learning? In the traditional classroom, the teacher is the sage from the stage, with all knowledge and content being handed out like a sermon on the mount. Students are being given what they need to know and they must figure out a way to remember it because they will have to apply it in an assignment or assessment. Problem-based learning turns the teacher into a guide from the side and the student is the one in control of the learning. The teacher is merely there to nudge the students should they get off course. Anything the students learn will be the result of their own work, meaning they have applied it before they ever get to the assignment or assessment, allowing them to take it even further and understand it better. It is the difference between passive and active learning. This active learning not only engages the students but also their minds.

The definition of problem-based learning

Now that we know the context of the pedagogy of problem-based learning, let's encapsulate this in a nice, tidy definition that will simplify but give you the general idea. According to the Center for Teacher Innovation at Cornell, PrBL:

> is a student-centered approach in which students learn about a subject by working in groups to solve an open-ended problem.

It is important though that we unpack these terms so that we have a full understanding of the elements of PrBL and how they work together as a whole. These key terms are:

- *Student-centered*: this means that students are the ones driving the car and making most of the decisions. This, of course, is the heart of inquiry learning. This involves a lot of student choice and autonomy. It also means that the role of the teacher changes drastically from that of a traditional classroom and finding one's place in such an environment can be an adjustment.
- *Working in groups*: you do not always have to have students working in groups but by doing so they will also be learning through this process the skill of collaboration. This is something that should be deliberately taught.
- *Open-ended problem*: there is a major difference between solving a problem and problem solving. When you solve a math problem, fix a grammatical problem, or you are solving a problem using scientific law, there is a right or wrong answer. Problem solving on the other hand is typically open-ended, which means there are multiple solutions to the same problem, any one of which could be viable. The best problems to pose to students are actually ones that do not have an answer. These are problems with no final solution and because of this, will get students to think even more.

You put these terms together into an actionable strategy by reversing the order of the definition:

> Problem-based learning poses an open-ended problem that students must try and solve collectively with others, being given much student choice and autonomy during the process.

This definition is all very well and good, but it is just that, a definition. It remains in theory. The logical question becomes what does this actually look like in the classroom.

What PrBL looks like in the classroom

What would this actually look like in practical application in the classroom? How do we turn this theory into practice? This is what it might look like in a social studies class:

> Egypt has a problem with land mines, having a reported 23 million of them scattered throughout its borders; 8000 people have died from injuries from land mines since the end of World War II. What can Egypt do to prevent more people from being harmed?

Students would research the problem and see if there are any viable solutions that have not been tried that would be possible. One of the students comes across an article about Magawa, an African giant pouched rat that has the uncanny ability to sniff out land mines. He works for an organization known as APOPO, which trains these specialized rats to help find land mines throughout Cambodia. Magawa by himself has discovered 109 explosives that have been disarmed and removed. Students would then figure out how to expand the program to include Egypt and develop a plan for what this would look like.

In math class students might be challenged with this dilemma:

> You are looking at three different games
> - Yahtzee
> - Bingo
> - War
>
> Which of these games has the greatest probability of:
> - You winning
> - Taking the shortest amount of time to finish
> - Taking the longest amount of time to finish
> - Skill causing you to win

Students would then have to determine for themselves such things as:

- Making sense of problems
- Reasoning abstractly and quantitatively

♦ Constructing viable arguments
♦ Modeling with mathematics
♦ Using appropriate tools such as diagrams

We can also take a traditional lesson, and with just a few tweaks, can transform it into a PrBL lesson:

Traditional classroom	Problem-based learning classroom
You are teaching a unit on poetry. You show them various forms and then assess whether they can identify them or not.	Have students study various forms of poetry and have them write a poem in a specific format or style.
Students learn about various geologic formations by reading about them in a book. They then must draw a poster that displays the various formations.	Students learn about various geologic formations and must help design a comic book that uses these to cause a dilemma that the hero must solve.
The civilization of Mesopotamia is studied with students learning the various contributions such as the city-state, the code of laws, and cuneiform.	Students must juxtapose what the world would be like if the Mesopotamians had never been around. What would change and why? What would our own country/community look like?
Solving problems to learn how to add and subtract decimals, specifically with money.	Given a budget, students must determine what they can buy at the grocery store in order to feed a family of five for an entire month.

You have to ask yourself, which of these activities seem to be more engaging for students? Which of them is most likely going to enable students to find the relevance of what they are learning and how it works in the real world? Which of them is going to yield an interesting assessment to show whether they mastered the content or not? Which is going to challenge student thinking?

Do we have a problem here?

PrBL is one of the strategies that uses the inquiry-learning process. This involves the students being a major player in the direction the learning is going by asking questions, investigating these questions through research or other sources, and creating a product that shows mastery of what was learned through this process that is then discussed and reflected upon. Because of its focus on the process, students are learning all sorts of different things from one another because each is going about it in a different manner. This is what allows the learning to be personalized as well as relevant to students because they get to decide how this problem relates to their own lives. It makes for an authentic and engaging learning experience.

> **Activity #1**
> *Now that you know what PrBL is, create an explanation that could be used to give others a quick overview of what it is. This could be a PowerPoint, a YouTube video, an entry in Wikipedia, or some other product that forces you to break it down step-by-step in your explanation in order for others to understand. Think about what essentials people need to know and how you will show or demonstrate these.*

2

What are the Benefits of Problem-Based Learning?

> **Problem #2**
> *You are team-teaching with a colleague. You instruct social studies and ELA while he teaches science and math. You do this fairly independently of one another so you teach how you teach which is different than his more traditional manner. However, there are interdisciplinary lessons that use PrBL that would be even more effective if you taught them together. How do you convince this teacher to try this new trick? What benefits could you show him to make him see the value in teaching in such a way?*
>
> **Learning objectives:**
> - ★ What are the benefits of problem-based learning?
> - ★ Why do these benefits make it important that we use this teaching strategy?
> - ★ How do you convince someone to change the way they have always done things?

Chapter 1 mentioned several benefits that can result from using problem-based learning in your classroom. However, this chapter seeks to make a clear-cut, air-tight case as to the benefits PrBL can have on you and your students, and how in today's learning environment you cannot afford not to use it.

DOI: 10.4324/9781003302605-3

Why teach with PrBL?

What is the purpose of teaching? In its simplest form, the point is for people to learn. But there is more to it than that. How is learning being defined? Is it the memorization of facts? Is it a deeper understanding? And how long does the learning last? Do students forget it after a week or a month? Do students remember it the following year or even years?

Think about your own life. What learning has been most meaningful to you? Usually, it is learning that you have been able to use in your adult life, learning that you remembered long after you left the classrooms of your school. How do we get that kind of enduring learning with our students?

There are a few things that problem-based learning provides that gives students a better chance at such lifelong learning:

- Since the problems introduced are typically open-ended questions with no clear-cut or correct answer, this provides lots of space for discussions, debates, and comparisons. In order to support these positions and make an argument, students need to truly understand the concept as well as collecting evidence to make their case.
- Because PrBL has a focus on application rather than a simple recall of facts, this helps in the retention of knowledge for the long term. Students must find solutions to real-life problems, giving them the context to understand how it fits into the world they live in and better understand it.
- Students do most of the learning themselves with just occasional guidance from the teacher. Because students are forming the questions, finding the necessary research and evidence, and figuring out a way to present these findings, they discover how to learn for themselves and this creates independence. Students no longer have to wait for the teacher to tell them what to learn. Students can decide for themselves what they want to learn. It gives them initiative.
- One of the best things about PrBL, especially in regard to gifted children, is it promotes higher-order thinking skills. They will be analyzing, evaluating, and creating on a daily basis rather than the remembering, understanding, and applying of the traditional classroom. Because the problem is open-ended, there are many possibilities, meaning each group might come up with a different solution using a different thought process. But if the problem is an authentic one, the possible solution will not be the most obvious one but rather

one that requires them to dig a little deeper. And because they are learning independently, students are using independent thinking.
- Finally, because PrBL is authentic, students must use authentic skills in order to be successful. The more authentic the skill, the more transferable this will be to their own lives. For example, if a student learns how to research statistics on air pollution in Beijing, China, this skill can be transferred when he needs to use it in his real life such as when he is trying to find a reasonably priced car or how to start a small business. These skills are relevant because they can be used outside of the four classroom walls and in students' actual lives. As to what some of these transferrable skills are, we will take a look at specific ones in the next section.

After hearing what sort of learning can result from PrBL, ask yourself whether it is the sort of learning your students would benefit from.

21st-century skills

Battelle for Kids, an organization with the mission of realizing the power and promise of 21st century learning for all students, defines 21st-century skills as ones that ask that "all students have an educational experience preparing them to be effective lifelong learners and contributors." These so-called "soft skills" are hard to measure in the classroom but are invaluable in the real world.

There are hundreds of these soft skills from time management and empathy to decisiveness and a sense of humor. Tony Wagner in his book *The Global Achievement Gap* defined these further when he termed them "survival skills." These were seven skills that every young person entering the workforce should have in order to be highly successful. These soft skills are:

- Critical thinking/problem solving
- Collaboration
- Adaptability
- Initiative
- Effective oral/written communication
- Accessing and analyzing information
- Curiosity (Wagner, 2008)

When you look at the traditional method of teaching, which is the teacher disseminating information that students learn and then must show mastery on an assessment, they are not hitting many of these skills. Sure, you could make an argument for initiative if students get their homework turned in on time or effective written communication if students are answering essay questions. But the other skills of critical thinking, curiosity, and adaptability would not be a part of the regular classroom practice, they would have to be forced into the classroom culture.

What if instead you could use a teaching strategy that uses not just a couple, but all seven skills in a very organic manner? That would be problem-based learning:

- Critical thinking and problem solving: considering this is called problem-based learning, problem solving is what it is all about. The open-endedness of the problem itself with its multiple possibilities will require students to think critically, weighing options for solutions and going with the one that makes the most logical sense.
- Collaboration: being a part of the inquiry structure, students learn how to successfully work with others. Because in their lives they will have to learn how to work with others, whether it be in their home, at their work, or amongst their friends, it is so important that students understand how to do this. Developing coping mechanisms and strategies for when things become difficult provides students with a toolbox that they can use anytime something similar comes along.
- Adaptability: this is one's ability to change in midstream. When things don't go as planned, do you have the ability to pivot to plan B, C, or D? You know, life. People who lack the ability to adapt, especially in the 21st century where technology is changing all of the time, usually find themselves left behind. Because problem-based learning is open-ended, there is no one correct answer and because of this, there is the possibility of many avenues, some of which are dead ends, others that go on forever with no end in sight. But students need to learn how long to stay on that road. They have to be able to explore a path and then switch to another if it doesn't seem to be yielding any fruit.
- Initiative: because a good amount of the responsibility of learning is put back on the students, they will need to learn how to manage time, make choices of where to take the learning, and determine for themselves how far and deep they want to take it. This is certainly a valuable lifelong skill because when you get out into the real world, there is no one there requiring you to read books, no one who is monitoring your progress along the way to ensure success, no one to hand you the information you need, nor is there anyone to encourage you to learn. If you want to learn, you have to do it on your own. The

independence PrBL affords encourages students to show initiative in their own learning, which increases their motivation.
- Effective oral and written communication: because performance assessments are the norm for showing mastery of problem-based learning, there are lots of opportunities for students to develop and improve their oral and written communication. Students might decide to create a portfolio, write a research paper, capture thoughts and ideas in a journal, or other forms of written communication. In doing so, students must learn the purpose of written communication, which is to clearly inform. Other options might be presenting to an authentic audience, filming a video, giving a speech, taking part in a debate, or some other oral presentation. Each time a student takes part in one of these, he is gaining the confidence to speak in public and understand how to communicate in this fashion.
- Accessing and analyzing information: research is a crucial component of problem-based learning. This is how students gather the evidence to make a case for solving their problem. Being able to access and analyze this information is going to be really important for students to find reliable resources that make this case strong. This will be a vital skill for them to have in their adult lives. Being able to read or watch something and discern for yourself what is fact, what is opinion, and whether this seems reputable or not will help you in making better decisions, whether it is politics, a movie review, or to invest in something.
- Curiosity: this would seemingly be an easy one. After all, children are born curious creatures. They want to explore everything, try anything, and ask millions of questions to have their thirst for curiosity whetted. There is nothing we have to do to nurture this. However, schools do a pretty good job of quashing this. Studies have shown the longer students are in school, the less engaged they become, and their innate curiosity gets replaced by resentment that they have to do it. Problem-based learning is designed to get students to love learning again. It encourages them to ask questions and explore their ponderings. It allows them to look under metaphorical rocks, open metaphorical doors, and travel down metaphorical pathways. This is all part of the process of learning spoken about in the introduction of this book. PrBL doesn't give students curiosity, it simply allows them to use what they already possess.

It is the combination of these skills that creates these global citizens who can successfully go out into the world and be successful

Its place in the workplace and beyond

To prove to you the importance of such skills being coveted out in the real world, here is some evidence to show what is important to employers. According to *Forbes*, the top ten skills being sought in 2020 are:

1. Accessing and analyzing data
2. Critical thinking
3. Tech savviness
4. Adaptability
5. Creativity
6. Emotional intelligence
7. Cultural diversity
8. Leadership skills
9. Problem solving
10. Collaboration

You see a lot of those survival skills in this list.

When the University of Phoenix asked employers for the top skills they are looking for in potential employees, the top five were:

1. Critical thinking
2. Ability to learn new skills
3. Collaboration
4. Accessing and analyzing information
5. Communication skills (Fairbanks, 2021)

Even the international market reflects these 21st-century skills. This was a list of skills Chinese employers were looking for when recruiting potential employees (Global Fitness for Work, n.d.):

Even jobs in the future reflect the need for these important survival skills. A projection of the skills companies will be looking for in 2025 by the World Economic Forum is as follows (World, 2020):

Top 10 skills of 2025
• Analytical thinking and innovation
• Active learning and learning strategies
• Complex problem-solving
• Critical thinking and analysis
• Creativity, originality, and initiative
• Leadership and social influence
• Technology use, monitoring and control
• Technology design and programming
• Resilience, stress tolerance, and flexibility
• Reasoning, problem-solving and ideation

If we are hoping to provide students with a chance to compete in the job market once they leave school, we cannot just be preparing them for jobs that currently exist, but those that have not even been thought of yet. Lots of skills become obsolete but these survival skills taught through problem-based learning are timeless.

Student motivation

It seems to be getting harder and harder to motivate students. A 2015 Gallup Poll showed that the longer students are in school, the less engaged and motivated they are:

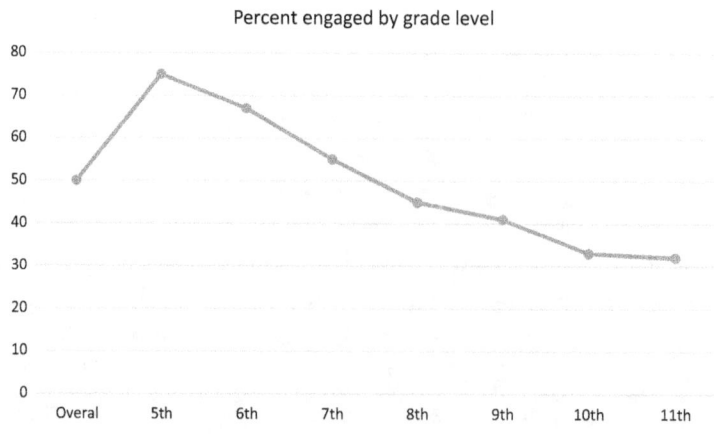

There are many contributing factors to this loss of motivation from too many teacher-centered classrooms and the reliance on memorization of content, to the lack of personalization, with some teachers being responsible for over 150 students, making it difficult to cultivate a relationship in the 45 minutes they have them in class. One of the biggest issues is the focus on extrinsic motivation such as grades and GPA, and less focus on intrinsic motivation.

Intrinsic motivation is learning for the sake of learning, not because there is some shiny prize that awaits you should you complete the task. The task instead is completed because in doing so you are learning something that you think is worthwhile. This is the type of learning that leads to creative and higher-order thinking. This is the learning that sticks with students. It is also the sort of learning that leads to complex problem solving. But how do we instill this intrinsic motivation in students? One such idea is the self-determination theory which involves the following elements:

- Autonomy: students need to have a degree of control over what needs to happen and how it can be done.
- Competence: effective feedback increases students' intrinsic motivation and the feeling that they have the ability to be successful.
- Relatedness: relevant activities make students feel more connected to others and feel cared about by people they respect.
- Relevance: students must see work as interesting or valuable to them, and useful to their present lives and/or hopes and dreams for the future.

If only there were a teaching strategy that allowed one to include all of these elements. Oh wait, there is this thing called problem-based learning. PrBL has been shown to be:

- Highly engaging
- Encourages intrinsic rewards
- Students with PrBL experience rate their abilities higher and have more confidence
- Can better see how the learning fits into their own lives
- Promotes a love of learning

Why is increased motivation important besides the very obvious? The Center of Educational Policy at George Washington University put together a report that states:

> Higher motivation to learn has been linked not only to better academic performance, but to greater conceptual understanding, satisfaction

with school, self-esteem, and social adjustment, and to lower dropout rates. Not only is student motivation the final piece of the school improvement puzzle — without it, the rest of the puzzle falls apart.

(Motivation, 2016)

Benefits to the teacher

Like any human being, what you might be wondering at this point is this all sounds good, but what is in it for me? This is a perfectly normal thought and there are some pretty attractive benefits for the person teaching using PrBL.

One of the most important is that not only is this sort of learning engaging for the students, but it is also engaging for the teacher as well. Standing up in front of the class all day long and spewing out information can be exhausting as well as boring. How many times have you gotten to that fifth class at the end of the day and thought to yourself, "didn't I already say this?" PrBL frees you from the shackles of the front of the classroom and allows you to move around the room and have conversations with students about their learning. You will learn more from these one-on-one talks than most assessments can show you. It also allows you to challenge the thinking of students by posing questions and then walking away and watching it marinate in their heads. It is this extra-added push that is going to raise the rigor in your class, not how difficult the questions are. And having to assess 150 essays or grade multiple choice tests is not the most exciting way to spend your time either. Because there are choices, students will often choose alternative assessments such as presentations, portfolios, and models to name a few. These are so much more interesting to evaluate because you can see the learning and the excitement that went into them. It also breaks up the monotony of doing the same thing over and over by providing some variety.

Another advantage is that the onus of the work is placed on the students rather than the teacher. In a typical classroom, you are doing most of the heavy lifting from the planning to the dissemination of what was found, to the assessment of this understanding. PrBL allows for all of this to be done by the students. After all, they are the ones in school, they are the ones that are supposed to do the learning. Should they not be doing the bulk of the work? Besides the advantage to yourself, it makes them self-directed learners who show initiative for their own education. You are creating lifelong learners by using a strategy such as PrBL.

Because problem-based learning teaches the aforementioned survival skills, these are lifelong skills that can be used in any situation, academic or otherwise. Think back to your own schooling. How much do you remember of content as compared to skills? You probably don't remember the seven animal kingdoms, the Pythagorean Theorem, the 11th Amendment, or what exactly a modifier does. This is because you don't use these in your everyday life and therefore that knowledge has been tucked away in some neglected part of your brain. However, you analyze information all the time, whether it be figuring out where to buy a house, where to go on vacation, or whether eating that extra piece of chocolate cake will ruin your diet. You must use effective oral communication when talking with your boss, your family, or the contractor who you are trying to explain what you want your basement to look like. And problem solving? Life is full of problems to solve so having the coping mechanism to handle these when they come your way is going to give you an advantage, whether it be trying to figure out how you are going to get your kid to school while at the same time going to your morning meeting, or how on earth you are going to remove the tree that has died in your yard. As a teacher, wouldn't it be satisfying to know that what you are teaching will be used down the road? You can almost guarantee this with problem-based learning as your main teaching pedagogy.

Any teacher who has been in the business for very long knows that the key to student learning is the teacher–student relationship. If the teacher does not engage with the student, it is difficult for the child to be motivated. Plus knowing the strengths and weaknesses of your students gives you an advantage in knowing how best to work with them. PrBL enriches the teacher–student relationship because it frees you up from the front of the classroom and provides you with the time to sit down and talk individually with students. These conversations could be about the schoolwork they are currently doing in your class, what their prior knowledge on the topic might be, or how their life in general is going.

Finally, it can often feel as though you are teaching in a silo. Students enter your room and once the door is closed, no one really knows what goes on behind it nor do you get to see what anyone else is doing. This can sometimes be a nice thing but often it is lonely. The profession of teaching is one that lends itself to colleagues and collaboration. Problem-based learning lends itself to cross-curricular learning. Take this problem for example:

> The community playground would like to make itself more accessible to people with a disability. It would like to see playground equipment that children in wheelchairs would be able to use. With a budget of $10,000, figure out what you could do to improve the playground for those with disabilities. You will be presenting this to the city council for consideration.

There are a lot of subject areas that could be covered by this one PrBL assignment. There is the obvious social studies that has to do with improving the community, geography, and good citizenship. There is of course math in figuring out the budget of what you can and cannot spend money on. There is the ELA aspect of research and writing the speech you will give to the city council. There is the science of whether some of the ideas they have will even be physically possible (can you make a slide that works for wheelchairs). You could create this project together with other teachers who share your students, each looking at a different aspect that relates to their subject area, but the students would see as a whole how all of the subject areas work together to solve this one problem. Because PrBL is so wide in its ideas and involves the real world, it would be easy to create lessons together with other teachers, allowing for collaborations with colleagues.

Disadvantages of PrBL

There are some very real concerns a teacher might have concerning problem-based learning, but many of these are frightening only because they are unfamiliar. Some people do not like to be out of their comfort zone and PrBL would certainly pull them out of theirs. This type of authentic learning is so different than what is being done in most classrooms. There is often no one to turn to in order to see what it should look like or to get guidance from. But as teachers, we have to be willing to practice what we preach. We cannot ask students to learn something new that takes them out of their comfort zone unless we are willing to do the same. We cannot expect students to take risks if we are afraid to take them ourselves. And we cannot hope for them to be open-minded if we ourselves are being closed.

A lot of the arguments against PrBL are often misconceptions because we simply do not know what it will be like because we haven't done it before. For example, one very real constraint that teachers face on a daily basis is having enough time. As teachers, we are responsible for cramming in an overwhelming number of content standards that our students will be held accountable for at the end of the year. For every pep rally, snow day, fire drill, and teacher in-service day, we are losing precious time with our students, time that we cannot get back. How on earth can we possibly try problem-based learning, which is asking us to stop the drill and kill, and instead let the students call the shots and explore? In addition, it can be more time-consuming to grade the products that result from PrBL, which often are performance-based assessments.

The question teachers need to ask themselves is whether it is better to cover a ton of material that students understand on a basic level, or to go a little more in-depth and allow students to develop an enduring understanding? Not to mention that one problem-based learning lesson can address a number of content standards. Properly managed, you can turn your content standards into problems that students will solve rather than the information they will simply get. It is through this discovery of learning that they will better retain what is learned.

Another disadvantage is the fact that your students are not used to PrBL. They have spent a good majority of their schooling career having decisions made and content provided for them. Imagine how difficult it would be now that you are suddenly giving them choices and asking them to find what they need for themselves. This can be remedied by a proper introduction to problem-based learning. Don't start a PrBL lesson on the first day of school. Start by building skills they might need to successfully work on PrBL. Once students have learned these skills, they will feel a lot more comfortable when it comes time to use them.

Assessments will look very different in a PrBL classroom. Students may not be working on the same thing, meaning there will be all sorts of different ways students will need to be assessed. And because the problems are open-ended, there is no one correct answer for the teacher to evaluate. There can be a bit of subjectivity and it might be difficult to grade with an exact score. Most of these problems can be solved with student-created rubrics. If you are going to make students a part of the learning process, you need to go all in and allow them to decide how they will be assessed as well. This does a couple of things. 1) It allows them to have a say in how they will be graded, making them have ownership of the learning. 2) It also creates less work for yourself because students will be writing the rubric instead of you. This way the rubric will be personalized. Of course you will have to spend some time showing them how to write an objective rubric.

Along with this is the management of the classroom. Problem-based learning looks a whole lot different than your typical or traditional classroom. If you try and run your classroom like those, you will find it difficult. Instead, you need to rethink the way a classroom is organized because now it is the students who are calling the shots. A large part of this is relinquishing control of the classroom, but not the management of it. This can be a difficult thing to get used to and will be discussed in a lot more detail in Chapter 9 on the role of the teacher.

A final disadvantage that some might use as an excuse not to do problem-based learning is the anxiety it causes because the learning is messier, both for students and for the teacher. Of course, that is the point; that problems in the real world are not these tidy issues with a single correct answer. Problems in the real world can have many possible answers and you can make the correct one and it still does not work out. A PrBL classroom looks like chaos, but it is organized chaos. Students have a purpose – they just aren't all synchronized together like some traditional classrooms can be. You and your students need to be prepared for this chaos and understand that it is part of the process. It will certainly get easier with time.

Part of the anxiety can also be caused by the fact that often students are working in groups that can be messy as well. Developing norms and coping systems to make this process more effective can go a long way in easing this fear.

Do we have a problem here?

There are many benefits to using problem-based learning as a teaching strategy in your classroom. The big question to ask yourself though is do you find any of these compelling enough to give it a try in your own classroom? If not, you probably shouldn't do it. The purpose of using PrBL as an instructional strategy is not to attempt something new or because you are told to, it is because you feel it is what is best for kids. If it is not, find something else that you believe fits this bill. We all bring strengths as teachers that are different from others. If you do not feel you could ever pull off PrBL, it is going to be very difficult to do so with integrity. If, however, you are open-minded and willing to give it a try, read on. You will be shown step-by-step on how you can do this in your classroom and the places where you can make it your own. One PrBL classroom does not necessarily look like another, there is no one correct way to roll this strategy out. However, there are elements that you need to be aware of that serve as the foundation.

> **Activity #2**
> *Make a list of the reasons why you might be hesitant to use problem-based learning. Then determine whether these reasons are genuine or if they simply require a better understanding through research or exposure. Much like you would ask students to do with PrBL, explore these issues and develop a solution to each of them. If after doing so you still are not sure, determine for yourself whether you can live with these issues or whether PrBL is just not for you.*

3

Steps to Problem-Based Learning

> **Problem #3**
> *You have been asked to explain to someone who has never done so before, how to brush their teeth. It is important that you do not skip any details. For example, you cannot assume they know how to even put toothpaste on the toothbrush. Or you cannot tell them to brush their teach without warning them not to swallow.*
>
> **Learning objectives:**
> ★ How many steps will it take you to do so?
> ★ How much detail do you need to include in each step?
> ★ How do you teach something to someone and make sure you are not overlooking any important steps?

A big misconception of PrBL is that because students are the ones supposedly in charge, there is no structure. On the contrary, without a structure, PrBL will collapse on itself. Much like a house, there needs to be a solid one in place or nothing will be able to stand. You will want to be sure to build the lesson around this structure You or your students can certainly add things to this and make modifications, but underneath it will be the six basic steps that will be discussed in this chapter.

DOI: 10.4324/9781003302605-4

The steps of problem-based learning

When using problem-based learning in the classroom, there are certain steps to go through. These steps are:

1) Present the problem
2) List what is known
3) Develop a problem statement
4) List what is needed/ask questions
5) List actions, solutions, or hypothesis
6) Present and support the solution

These will be talked about in more detail as the chapter goes on but one decision you have to make as the teacher is how much control over each of these are you allowing. For example, are you giving students all aspects of the problem or are you giving them a part of it and then letting them decide which direction they want to go with it? You could have the problem be as specific as this:

> There is a TikTok challenge known as Devious Licks that has encouraged students to vandalize bathrooms, doing things such as taking soap dispensers, cracking tiles, or using graffiti.

Or you could make it more general:

> Following the rules at our school?

This more general problem gives students a lot of choices. They could tackle the problem of the use of cell phones in the classroom, running in the hallways, truancy, vandalism of school property, chewing gum, and so on.

When it comes to the problem statement, are you providing this for students or are you letting them develop it themselves? Using our example from before, you might want students to specifically look at the problem in the bathrooms so you might offer this problem statement:

> What should the school do about protecting the bathrooms from the TikTok Devious Licks challenge?

Students might decide to handle this in a multitude of ways:

- How do we prevent the vandalism of our bathrooms?
- How do we inform others of the bad influence of TikTok?

- How do we teach overall good citizenship?
- How do we make students feel like part of the school community?
- How do we create countercampaigns on TikTok against the challenge?

Each one of these is a different variation of the same problem. Some are more specific while others are more systemic. You can see this provides students more opportunities to make the learning something relevant to themselves. Some students with a lot of school spirit might want to figure out how to help others have this pride in their school. Another who really likes TikTok takes on the task of making her own TikTok challenge, giving it a more positive spin and posting videos to promote it.

When it comes to presenting the solution, you might already have an authentic audience in place that you want the students to pitch to. For example, you have assembled members of the student council of the school to sit on a panel and your students will present their solutions to them. This means students did not have a whole lot of choice when it comes to the format. This obviously needs to be an oral presentation of some sort. Students could certainly vary it by adding a PowerPoint or creating a video, but the basic format will be the same.

If you gave students a choice in how they were going to present their solutions, some might:

- Create a PSA campaign with announcements and posters
- Help rewrite the school rules so there is consistent handling of the situation
- Form a student principal's advisory committee to handle problems such as this
- Make a TikTok challenge of your own that promotes taking care of your school
- Address the school board on how to best stop the problem of vandalism to our bathrooms

The point, if it hasn't hit you over the head by now, is the less control you have over each of the aspects, the more choices students are going to have for themselves. This student choice allows them to be more motivated because they are getting a say in how they are learning and being a part of the process. There may be times when you are looking for something very specific and thus you control that aspect. For the example used, you really want to build the skill of public speaking so that is why you should arrange to have an authentic audience (which is always a good idea) for student presentations.

Ultimately, the amount of control you give to your students is totally up to you. Do what feels comfortable for you and your students, and then as you use PrBL more and more, figure out ways to give up more control as you begin trusting your students and the both of you get used to how this structure can work.

Present the problem

This is what sparks the whole lesson. How can you take what you want students to learn and present it as a problem? Better yet, how can you have students reach this conclusion on their own and yet still include what you want it to? An example would be if you want to teach fractions to students. How do you, aside from making actual math problems, present this to students as a real-world problem? One way would be to present the following problem:

> You are hosting a birthday party. You have invited six guests. Your mom plans to order two large pizzas, each cut into eight slices. She also has made a cake that is eight inches in diameter. Taking what you have learned about fractions, make a guest list of real people you know and decide what is the fairest way to divide up the pizza and how big a piece of cake should each of the guests receive? Your answers should be in fractions. Be ready to explain your decisions.

Students would undoubtedly have to use fractions in order to figure this out, fractions of both pizza and the cake. There is some openness to the problem. The student gets to decide on the invited guests. One of these guests might be gluten free and thus will not have any of the pizza. Or a person might not like chocolate cake which is your favorite and what you are asking your mother to make for you so you get the biggest piece. We are going to continue to work on this problem throughout the chapter so you can see what an entire problem looks like when unfolding through the various steps.

No matter what the problem involves, whether it be fractions, Hammurabi's Code of Law, rocks and minerals, or foreshadowing in *The Lord of the Rings*, there are elements you will want to include:

- The initial steps of the problem should be open-ended and engaging to draw students into the problem
- The problem should require students to make reasoned decisions and defend them
- The problem should incorporate the content objectives in such a way as to connect it to previous courses/knowledge

- If used for a group project, the problem needs a level of complexity to ensure that the students must work together to solve it (Duch, Groh, and Allen, 2001)

When we look back at our fractions problem, does it include all of these elements?

- Open-ended because the student gets to pick the guests from real-life people
- Students must make decisions based on the amount of food and the guests invited and show the logic behind these
- Incorporating previous knowledge of fractions as well as building new ones
- Could easily be turned into a group assignment where students look at a larger party with more guests and food

Students could create all sorts of problems dealing with fractions. Some of these might include:

- Going clothes shopping at a store where there are all sorts of half and quarter off sales where they would have to figure out how much they would have to pay
- Creating a recipe that uses all sorts of fractions such as 1/3 cup of brown sugar, ¼ TBSP of vanilla, or 3/12 a carton of eggs
- Analyzing sports that use fractions such as basketball, baseball, or soccer
- Keeping track of their fitness by figuring out their body mass index as well as portions of food they eat on a daily basis
- Determining their final grades, figuring out what each assignment or aspect of grading weighed in the total score

Any one of these problems could be used to demonstrate mastery of fractions so you could have several groups working on several different problems.

List what is known

Once the problem has been either presented or created by the students, they need to list what is known. This is essentially unpacking the problem and all of its elements. This is based only on facts that have been presented in the problem. A list from our chapter example might look like this:

- Six guests have been invited
- Food includes two pizzas and an eight-inch cake
- Divide the food among the people at the party
- Answers should be in fractions

Some of these might be implied. For example:

- You are hosting the party so you need to be sure to include yourself in the count

But students should not interpret these facts. That will be done later in the process. Instead, the problem should be broken down and all of the known facts gleaned from it.

What a list such as this enables students to do is identify everything that must be mastered. It becomes a checklist that allows them not to overlook anything and to see everything that must be included.

Develop a problem statement

Once they have unpacked the information presented to them, students need to develop their problem statement. It is essentially the goal they hope to achieve by the end of their work. The problem is the question that is being asked, the problem statement is what the answer is going to look like. It is taking the question mark off of the problem and making a statement as to what is going to be done.

For the problem we have been working with, a problem statement might look like this:

> Figure out how to divide two large pizzas and one eight-inch cake among the seven guests that you have invited to your birthday party.

As you can see, all of the elements of the question have been captured in this statement. If students were to solve this statement, they would be answering the question that was posed to them.

List what is needed/ask questions

This is the point where students begin to assess exactly what needs to happen in order to be able to solve the problem. During this time, students will want to ask all sorts of questions, some of which can be answered, some which cannot. But stones should be unturned and all sorts of situations bandied about. This is the spot where a lot of outside-the-box thinking can occur. It might be difficult for the students to figure out how to put it back in the box so that it can be used to solve the problem, but you want them to do that sort of thinking. Every time the students ask a question, they need to determine whether it can be answered or not. If it cannot, they move on from it. If it can, they can use this to help solve the problem.

Questions that can be answered:
- Who is being invited to the party?
- Can you divide an eight-inch cake evenly into seven pieces?
- Would it be better to cut the cake into squares or triangles?
- Do any of the guests have dietary restrictions?
- Do any of the guests tend to eat more or less than others?
- What will the toppings on the pizzas be?
- How many pieces of pizza are there in total?
- Does food need to be distributed evenly?
- Are mom and dad included in the number of people eating?

Questions that cannot be answered due to constraints:
- What sorts of presents will people bring?
- Why doesn't mom just order another pizza?
- Could we take someone off the guest list?
- Can we cut the pieces of pizza into smaller pieces of pizza?
- Can I change the flavor of the cake?
- Can I use decimals instead of fractions?

Students use these questions to cover all aspects of the problem. Looking at several angles helps them see more than what is just in front of them.

List actions, solutions, or hypothesis

Once you have your questions, you can begin to develop answers for them. This will help students to determine the actions they will take to solve them.

- Who is being invited to the party?
  - Action: make a guest list
- Can you divide an eight-inch cake evenly into seven pieces?
  - Action: must figure out if this is possible

- Would it be better to cut the cake into squares or triangles?
  - Hypothesis: try it both ways and see which way distributes better
- Do any of the guests have dietary restrictions?
  - Action: check members of the guest list
- Do any of the guests tend to eat more or less than others?
  - Action: check guest list for ages and appetites
- What will my topping on the pizza be?
  - Hypothesis: which topping will more people like or not like?
- How many pieces of pizza are there in total?
  - Solution: 16
- Does food need to be distributed evenly?
  - Solution: no, some may eat more or less depending on their age and appetite
- Are mom and dad included in the number of people eating?
  - Hypothesis: try the equations with them included and not to see which works best

These answers create a checklist of things that need to be done in order to solve the problem. All of these need to be addressed in order to choose what is believed to be the best solution out of many possibilities.

Present and support the solution

Once you have gone through your checklist and considered all of the possible solutions, you must explain the one you chose, and more importantly, justify why that was the one you felt was the best. The form this answer takes can provide several choices and can be determined by the teacher or the students.

For instance, a teacher wants the students to work on being persuasive and providing details in writing, so he requests that students submit their solutions in written form. Or the teacher is trying to develop the 21st-century skill of public speaking so requires students to create a pitch video where they will orally present their solution and try to convince those watching why this would be the best choice.

If left up to the students, they might choose a method that bespeaks to a strength of theirs. If members of the group are skilled at graphic design, they may create a pamphlet that lays out their solution. Or perhaps they are very adept at coding so they decide to create a website that shows the solution.

They are many possibilities for how students show what they have learned; all you have to ensure is that whatever method they do use, it demonstrates mastery of the learning objectives you or they have set out. Remember, in PrBL, the product is not as important as it is for project-based learning. It is about the process (i.e., the steps) students have gone through to develop their solution where the real learning is taking place. But that does not mean you cannot have students develop specific skills as well as learning the lesson's objectives.

You could even make a menu/choice board where students are given multiple possibilities for how they want to represent their work and solution. For the fractions lesson, students might be given this:

Represent your solution in the form of pie charts that demonstrate the fractions used.	Enact your party live, providing the food, discussing how you are distributing the food, and why you have chosen to do it this way.
Form a debate with another group where you both try to persuade an impartial third party why your solution is better than the other solutions.	Film a YouTube video where you capture your thought process of the answers you developed and why you felt they were the best ones possible.

Students then could choose from any one of these to demonstrate what was learned.

Whenever possible, this solution should be given to an authentic audience. This does a few things:

- ◆ Brings it into the real world – not only is the problem you are solving a real-world one but the audience that is evaluating it is as well. These outside people bring their perspectives, their experiences, and their expertise into your classroom and provide context for what is being learned.
- ◆ Raises the stakes and expectations – presenting to a teacher or fellow classmates is a common occurrence. Presenting to strangers who are supposed "experts" means you really have to have your ducks in a row. Students tend to pay more attention to details and quality work because they want to impress these outsiders.
- ◆ Allows you to showcase what is going on in your classroom – many times we close our doors and no one sees the great things that are going on in our classrooms. But if you invite the superintendent in to act as an authentic audience member, find a parent who has expertise, or even community members, they might be amazed at what your students are doing.

How to bring authenticity to your PrBL will be discussed in further detail in Chapter 6.

Do we have a problem here?

Now you know the steps of problem-based learning. They are:

1) Present the problem
2) List what is known
3) Develop a problem statement
4) List what is needed/ask questions
5) List actions, solutions, or hypothesis
6) Present and support the solution

This structure allows students to follow the steps of PrBL and keeps their eyes focused on the prize. It acts as a tethering, allowing students to go off on all sorts of explorations but keeps them tied to the basic structure that they must follow. A student might go down a rabbit hole in their research, one thing leading them to another, but it is the structure that will bring them back to what the purpose of the lesson is. The students could look at the problem from several different angles, but ultimately, they need to be able to narrow it down to their problem statement. They might ask all sorts of questions, which then leads to other questions, which then leads to even further questions, but eventually, students must boil it down to an action or solution. This strong structure gives them the independence to become learners on their own while still moving them along for the purposes that you the teacher need to have them working toward.

It will be very important when using problem-based learning with your students that they understand these steps and what is the purpose of each of them. You as the manager of your classroom will need to remind them of these goals from time to time, whether on due dates, on syllabi, or verbally. This becomes the major task of the PrBL teacher, which will be discussed in much further depth in Chapter 9.

> **Activity #3**
> *Take a lesson that you already do and see how you can fit it into the steps of PrBL. What would need to be changed? What would need to be taken out or added? How easy a process was this? What other lessons could you do this with?*

4

Finding Big Hairy Problems

> **Problem #4**
>
> *You have been asked to solve a big hairy problem at your school. There are a lot of fights going on, office referrals, and general breaking of the rules. It isn't just one isolated incident – it seems to be affecting a lot more of the student body than in the past. It is like kids have forgotten how to do school.*
>
> **Learning objectives:**
>
> ★ Where will you start?
> ★ How will you find stakeholders in this process and communicate with them?
> ★ What is your step-by-step plan for fixing the culture of your school?

You want to use problem-based learning in your classroom so the first thing you need to do is find a problem. The good news is that there are lots of them out there. But more importantly, there are lots of problems that do not have easy solutions. In school, we teach students to find the correct answer, but in life, we know that often there is no correct answer, only choices. Some choices may be better than others but there is no clear-cut, definitive, correct answer that is going to solve all of your problems. That is what makes problem-based learning so real-world. And the best way to make it real-world is to make the problem a big hairy one.

DOI: 10.4324/9781003302605-5

What on earth makes a problem big and hairy?

When we are watching a movie or reading a book, the conclusion often ties up all loose ends and wraps the conflict into a nice little bow, with everyone living happily ever after. But what happens when Prince Charming and Cinderella begin to fight over whose turn it is to do the laundry? Or when Goldilocks is brought up on breaking and entering once the bears press charges? Or the psychiatric bills that pile up for Little Red Riding Hood in adulthood from the trauma of being attacked by the wolf at such a young age? Life doesn't end when the story does. It continues and often it can get messy. It is this messiness that makes things big and hairy.

Here is a perfect example of how history tends to try to make events clean, but when you actually dig a little deeper, you find that there is a big hairy messy problem underneath, the Civil War. The way we pitch this to students across the nation is that the South wanted slavery, but the North did not. Abraham Lincoln signed the Emancipation Proclamation, making slavery illegal in the United States and the South rebelled. The North fought and won to preserve the rights of all Americans to be treated as equals rather than as servants. Put more simply, slavery is bad, South supports slavery, South are the bad guys. North opposed slavery, North fought to free the slaves, North are the good guys.

Anyone who digs even just under the surface will find ginormous hairy problems. Among these would be:

- Some of the North wanted to expel Black people from the country altogether
- The South agrarian society depended on the slaves as workers so their motivation was financial
- Abraham Lincoln violated his executive branch power by signing the Emancipation Proclamation without the consent of Congress
- More about state rights than slave rights
- There are still ripple effects felt to this very day concerning racial equality

Any of these are plenty messy. There are probably entire books written on these particular issues.

Any one of these could be spun into a big hairy problem to be explored, analyzed, and commented upon.

What makes a big hairy problem? There are a few characteristics that a problem needs in order to be big and hairy:

- Does not have a definitive right or wrong answer
- Has the potential to break off into all sorts of other problems
- Can be taken on from many different angles and perspectives
- Is researchable
- Cannot be solved easily if at all

One that is super important from the perspective of the teacher is that the problem is researchable. What is meant by researchable is not that there are answers out there, it means that people who would be considered experts on this topic have collected information and data that students can use to make an informed decision. While there is a certain element of opinion in some of the answers that students may come up with, these opinions still need to be justified with evidence to strengthen them. This is why the answer the students give in their problem-based learning is not as important as their explanation of how they arrived at it. It is not the what of the answer, it is the why that is crucial for learning.

To provide you with an example of a big hairy problem that would be difficult to research would be one of the simplest problems that has been posed to humankind; which came first, the chicken or the egg? It certainly checks the boxes on the definition of a big hairy problem:

- Does not have a definitive right or wrong answer
- Has the potential to break off into all sorts of other problems
- Can be taken on from many different angles and perspectives
- Cannot be solved easily if at all

But there are no witnesses that were around when this event transpired, no YouTube footage, no primary documents that can be accessed, and no artifacts. In short, there is no research to be found. The only justification for either side would be based solely on opinion with no evidence to substantiate it. It is unresearchable. Thus, it is not a big hairy problem you would want to use for a PrBL lesson.

The more ethical the dilemma, the better

With that being said, another factor that makes problems big and hairy would be the ethical dilemma behind them. It is this that makes the problem gray as opposed to black and white. Let's take one of the most ethical dilemma endings in recent films. In the film *Gone Baby Gone*, the main character is hired as a private detective to find a little girl who has been abducted. Thinking she has been killed, he eventually finds her living with the very police captain who was heading up her investigation. It turns out her mother has been neglectful of her several times, even causing her to get severely sunburned from carelessness, and having lost his own child to abduction, the police captain thought he would save the little girl by taking her in as his own. The private detective is left with a decision; return the girl to her rightful mother, which would be putting her in danger from an unfit parent, or leave her with the loving family that unlawfully took her from her home. There is no easy answer, no noble act. Both decisions could end up being harmful to the girl or beneficial. There is no crystal ball to know which would be best. He certainly has a big hairy problem and complicating matters is that his girlfriend disagrees with the decision he makes, leaving him as a result. This is a decision you yourself would never want to find yourself having to make, which is what makes it so gosh darn interesting.

Part of the PrBL process is you want students to have to make difficult decisions. To understand what goes into making such a decision so when they are faced with one in their real lives, they are better equipped to handle it. This is going to be way more valuable to them than any content they learn.

There are all sorts of situations where ethical dilemmas raise their ugly head. There are:

- Personal relationships – falling in love with someone else while in a relationship with someone else.
- Life or death – having to sacrifice a life to save the lives of others.
- Following the rules – a player gets caught breaking the rules and the coach has to decide whether to let him play or not to play and possibly lose.
- The cost of a cure – can you put a price on a life because medicine does this all of the time, whether it be the cost of a life-saving surgery or the costs of expensive medication.
- Disadvantaging yourself to do what's right – you are willing to go to jail if it means not divulging the name of someone you are protecting.
- Good for the short term versus good for the long – it is a pain in the butt sometimes to recycle but we know by doing so that we will not be filling landfills.
- Justice versus mercy – letting someone live who has done something wrong to you because that is the law.

- Ethical leadership – when someone you respect does something unlawful, do you look the other way to keep them in leadership?
- Taking credit for someone else's work – you take credit for something someone else has done because it makes you look good.
- Lying to save face – do you tell someone the truth even though it might hurt their feelings or do you lie to prevent them from feeling bad?
- Invading someone's privacy to protect them – this would be looking at your child's phone to make sure they are being responsible.

One of the classic ethical dilemmas is the trolley car dilemma. In the situation, you are on a trolley car that is heading down a set of tracks. There are five people tied to the tracks in front of you but you could switch the track to one where there is only a single person. What do you do?

How about heightening the dilemma:

- What if the single person is a loved one of yours?
- What if the five people are members of the Ku Klux Klan?
- What if the single person is a small child and the five people are all elderly?
- What if you knew the single person would one day cure cancer?
- What if the five people are asking you to direct the car toward them?

These ethical dilemmas are dilemmas because there is no one correct answer. If you can find a problem for students that has an ethical dilemma, it makes it bigger and hairier and thus more interesting to dissect. Some examples of ethical dilemmas students could look at:

- Should we clone people to use them for transplant parts?
- Should Romeo have killed Tybalt to avenge the killing of his friend Mercutio?
- Should we send money to foreign countries to help others or should we use that money to help people in our own country?
- Should we consider the data and numbers when making a decision or should we be looking at the people and their faces?

There are tons of ethical dilemmas you could have your students look at. Just know that the murkier the ethics involved, the more interesting the problem and the more thinking students will have to do to create a solution for it.

The old reliable big hairy problems

As stated before, the world is full of problems and thankfully (or unthankfully depending on how you look at it) there are new ones all the time. However, there are some big hairy problems that have been around for a long time with no solution in the foreseeable future. These are:

- Energy
- Healthcare
- Environment
- Food and water
- Education
- Government
- Developing countries
- Economy
- Diversity
- Drugs

Any one of these would make a good topic for a PrBL. And you can make these problems as local or global as you need to.

For example, if you were looking at the big hairy problem of gifted education, you could look at several different levels concerning the issue:

- Local – how can you make sure students get enough time for gifted services in our school?
- District – how do we get the board of education to be willing to devote more resources to the enrichment of gifted students?
- State – how can we increase the identification in our state to include students who normally are not identified?
- Nation – how do we create a national standard for what it means to be gifted?
- World – how do we help countries that do not identify students as gifted to understand the importance of doing so?

You can see that the lens of this problem changes depending on what level you are looking at. Typically, the more local the problem, the more relevant it is to students because it is something that might directly affect them. But there are global issues that students feel very affected by as well, such as the environment and equality. You just need to decide or have the students themselves decide at what level you want to tackle a problem and which one will best align with the learning objectives you have for the lesson.

Ripped from the headlines

Because new problems are cropping up all of the time, you should be able to find something that is timely and relevant for students that can greatly aid in their motivation. It can be more meaningful to look at something that is currently happening as opposed to something that happened thousands or even hundreds of years ago. A glance through the daily headlines can produce a lot of problems to base lessons on.

On the day this was written, here are some of the headlines that could be found on news sites:

- Johnson and Johnson to split into two companies
- US journalist sentenced to 11 years in jail in Myanmar
- Rittenhouse trial sparks gun control culture
- Who could be legally responsible for the Astroworld tragedy?
- US warns that Russia could be planning to invade Ukraine

You can see that any one of these headlines could be developed into a problem.

- Johnson and Johnson to split into two companies
  - When does a company become too big?
- US journalist sentenced to 11 years in jail in Myanmar
  - Why don't all countries have freedom of the press?
- Rittenhouse trial sparks gun control culture
  - How do we prevent gun violence?
- Who could be legally responsible for the Astroworld tragedy?
  - Is an artist responsible for the actions of his/her fans?
- US warns that Russia could be planning to invade Ukraine
  - How does the world resolve conflicts between nations?

And here are some from the local news on that same day that could be developed into problems:

- Police, troopers are seeing drivers hit excessive speeds
  - How do we keep drivers from speeding?
- Armed teachers bill passes out of Ohio House Committee
  - Should teachers be allowed to carry a gun?
- Americans pile up nearly 30 pounds of extra trash
  - How can we cut down on the amount of trash we produce?

- Ohio Department of Health talks vaccines for children 5–11
  - What is the difference between vaccines for adults and those for younger children?
- Ohio lawmaker seeks expansion of medical marijuana law
  - What drugs should be legalized and why?

You as the teacher could either develop these problem statements or you could simply assign students to read the article and develop their own problem statement. For example, many problems could be gleaned from this headline:

- Gas prices are at a seven-year high

After students have listed what is known from the article, they could brainstorm possible problem statements.

- What causes gas prices to go up?
- How can we keep gas prices lower?
- Should we find an alternative to gas-powered automobiles?
- What happens when the world runs out of oil?
- What are the patterns or trends of gas prices?

You could go on and on. Students would then either choose the one that is most interesting to them or the most researchable, or the teacher might assign one of these possibilities because she might have a very specific idea that students need to explore.

Basing the problem on a content standard(s)

One problem that you might have is that you have to teach specific standards and are accountable for student mastery of these. Something to consider in order to ensure students are learning the specific standard is simply basing the problem on the content standard itself. In other words, turn the standard into a problem.

Let's take for example this common core ELA standard:

> Analyze how complex characters (e.g., those with multiple or conflicting motivations) develop over the course of a text, interact with other characters, and advance the plot or develop the theme.

This could be coupled with a book that the class is reading to analyze and put students in the shoes of a very complex character. You then have students try and solve the problem this complex character is dealing with. You would have to make sure that the answer is not provided later in the book or series so that students would have to develop their own. A problem might look like this:

> Imagine you are Severus Snape from the *Harry Potter* series. How difficult would it be to like Harry Potter given your feelings for Harry's parents? How do feel about being portrayed as an antagonist for most of the series when in fact you are a protagonist? How does this develop over the course of the series? How do your actions in the book justify your motivations? Considering all of these, make a case that you are a "gift of a character" as Rowling herself described you.

Students would then have to develop a case. This could be a mock trial, a video confessional, an essay, a slide presentation, a debate, an interview, and many other possibilities for a final product. You have provided a lot of guidance in this problem, leading students through the various aspects of the standard, but if you feel confident that your students could develop these on their own, you might simplify the problem:

> Make a case that you, Severus Snape, are a "gift of a character" as Rowling herself described you in the Harry Potter series.

Students would then develop the problem while following the steps to PrBL:

1) List what is known
2) Develop a problem statement
3) List what is needed/ask questions

Here is a Next Generation Science standard that could be turned into a problem:

> Evaluate competing design solutions using a systematic process to determine how well they meet the criteria and constraints of the problem.

You could pick any two designs and have students discern which one meets the problem better. For example, an iPhone compared with another smartphone, a Mac versus a PC, or Elon Musk's Falcon Heavy rocket as opposed to Jeff Bezos' Blue Origin. The possibilities are endless and students can choose any two design solutions that they feel passionate about.

This Common Core math standard could lead to many possible problems:

> Understand that statistics can be used to gain information about a population by examining a sample of the population; generalizations about a population from a sample are valid only if the sample is representative of that population. Understand that random sampling tends to produce representative samples and support valid inferences.

Students could conduct explorations of a population at local, national, or global levels:

Local: look at the last election for city council. Identify a population that was underrepresented in the voting. How do we as a city motivate those people to be involved in local elections?
Nation: analyze the population of Native Americans in the United States and how they are dispersed across the nation. How does this compare to how they were dispersed when Europeans first arrived? What patterns and inferences can you draw about the difference between the two?
Global: find out how much the population on our planet has increased in the past 50 years. What do you notice about this trend? Where are the largest pockets of growth in the world? If that pattern continues, what will the population be in 50 years? What can we do about the potential of over-population and where do you think it will be the worst?

It is fairly simple to take most content standards and turn them into a PrBL lesson because most of them are written as problems. By doing so, you will ensure that students still get the benefits of working on problem-based learning while making sure that the content standards they need to know for the state assessment are mastered.

Do we have a problem here?

As you have seen, problems are everywhere. It is not difficult to find them, you just need to make sure they are big and hairy so that students are challenged. Using problems that have an obvious answer or lack ethical ambiguity is not really problem-based learning, it is solving problems. If we truly want to get our students ready for the real world, they need to understand that problems often do not have an easy answer. The world can be a messy place so equipping students with the ability to take on these problems and having a structure to develop a plan for doing so is going to help them not only in school but in their everyday lives.

> **Activity #4**
>
> *Think of a big hairy problem in your own life. It can be work related, personal, or global. You are probably never going to be able to solve this problem, but you can certainly find ways to make things better. What information would you need to gather to make the most educated decision possible? How will this inform your decision? Consider then the what if? What if you try another solution? And then another? And another? Run through all of the possible scenarios including the best and worst cases for each decision. Is there any easy answer? Congratulations, you have now discovered what is meant by a big hairy problem.*

5
Grading the Process

Problem #5

You notice that your students are learning a lot as they go through the process of problem-based learning. This might be figuring out how to do effective research, collaborating with others well, overcoming a roadblock, or using critical thinking. You want to be able to capture mastery of this learning but traditional methods of assessment don't work. You can't give a multiple-choice test on collaboration, you can't measure perseverance on paper. How do you give your students credit for mastery in learning while in the process of learning?

Learning objectives:

★ What are some alternative assessments that could be used to capture this learning?
★ How do I make teacher observation a measurable assessment rather than just subjective?
★ How do I get students involved in the process of assessing themselves?

As stated in Chapter 1, the place where the most learning occurs in PrBL is in the process itself. Given that this is the case, how do you evaluate what students are learning during this process? Ideally, there would be a single assessment that would take a snapshot of that moment and that is how we would determine mastery? That is the problem though, that one snapshot does not necessarily give you an accurate portrayal of what students have learned in a PrBL lesson. We must consider multiple methods of assessment and types of assessments that capture what is being learned while it is occurring. It is best to create a toolbox of assessments that are good at doing this and then choosing the correct tool for the correct job. In other words, if a student demonstrates mastery through a conversation you are having, you must choose an assessment that would be good at capturing this. However, if they demonstrate mastery through some sort of writing assignment, you must have a different assessment to record this.

This chapter will seek to provide you with tools you might consider. One of the challenges of using these tools is that they take a lot more time and effort, both in their creation and in the grading of them. It would be so much easier to create a multiple-choice test with only a single answer that you could grade in just a few minutes. This is certainly an easy way to assess students, but few would argue that it is the most effective method. Yet students are evaluated on year-end state tests that are a majority of multiple-choice or take college entrance exams such as the ACT or SAT where they must boil down what they have learned into a single letter. These are easier to grade, which is why these testing companies use this method, but there are limits. A multiple-choice test is great if you are trying to measure knowledge. You can certainly write an excellent multiple-choice test to determine if students have memorized the facts. However, in the world today where you can ask your phone any knowledge question and likely get an answer, how valuable is this skill? Are there not more valuable skills we should be teaching our children as well as measuring? A multiple-choice test is going to have difficulty evaluating grit, perseverance, creativity, problem solving, collaboration, and other valuable skills that we want our students to possess. Should we not choose an assessment for measuring a skill appropriately instead of trying to fit a square peg into a round hole?

Tools for grading the process

When grading the process, it is important that you use assessments that can hit a moving target. What is meant by this is when the moment a student achieves understanding, it might not necessarily be neat or easy to capture on a traditional assessment. It might be something he says in a conversation, it could be something he demonstrates, it may be an end product, it could be something he discovers on his own. There must be methods for capturing this information so that mastery can be determined.

This chapter will cover seven different types of assessments that can be used to grade the process. Keep in mind, that these are not the only methods for assessing mastery, but they give you a foundation for what these assessments might look like and how to create them for your own classroom. These are:

- Use of rubrics
- Power of observation
- Evaluating discussions
- Student reflection
- Capturing conversations
- Portfolios
- Self and peer evaluations

Each one of these will be explained as to why it should be used, when you should use it, how it is used, and what it may look like.

Use of rubrics

Rubrics are wonderful tools for grading performance assessments because if written well, they show you and the students what it looks like. For example, if a student is giving an oral presentation. You might have a rubric that looks like the example on page 53.

Using this rubric, you should be able to capture the moment the student demonstrates these qualities and evaluate the level of mastery.

The importance of a rubric is that it clearly *shows* the evaluator what the act looks like at various levels. You can see the example rubric when it comes to evaluating the skill of speaking. This is shown at three different levels of performance:

- Accomplished – speakers present clearly consistently throughout and do not read to the audience.
- Average – speakers present clearly most times, reading to the audience only occasionally.
- Below average – speakers do not present clearly, often reading to the audience.

Anyone who has ever heard a presentation has seen all three of these levels and knows the difference. This is not something a student could demonstrate on a paper to pencil test. She might be able to write in an essay what it should look like but does that mean she can actually do it? This is the difference between theory and practice; rubrics are able to evaluate the practice.

	Overall	Presentation
Accomplished	**Accomplished**	• Speakers present clearly and consistently throughout, do not read to audience • Everyone is clear on what their role is and transitions between learning outcomes are smooth. • Presentation is organized in a professional manner, making it easy to follow what is being discussed at any given time.
Average	**Average**	• Speakers present clearly most times, reads to audience only occasionally. • Most everyone is clear on what their role is but there are some transitions between learning outcomes that could be more smooth. • Presentation is organized, making it easy to follow what is being discussed, but not as professional as could be.
Below average	**Below Average**	• Speakers do not present clearly, often reading to the audience. • It seems people are not clear on what their role is and transitions between learning outcomes are cumbersome. • Presentation is not organized, making it difficult to follow what is being discussed at any given time.

The limitations of rubrics can come in the fact that they are typically used in a summative fashion. Students are assigned tasks to complete and the rubric assesses whether they did them or not at the end of the lesson. How do we use rubrics while grading the process where mastery could be shown at any time? You design rubrics to monitor progress. Here is an example:

Indicate a spot on the spectrum by putting the date on the line in an appropriate place

Adaptability	Exceeding	Meeting	Progressing
Explore and Experiment	Eagerly takes on new challenges, has the initiative to learn independently, and tries innovative approaches to tasks.	Takes on new challenges, is willing to learn independently, and tried varied approaches to the tasks.	Takes on assigned challenges, is willing to learn independently, will vary approaches to tasks from time to time.
⬅			
Work effectively through changing priorities	Proactively anticipates challenges and potential changes, is able to overcome obstacles by being innovative.	Independently will anticipate challenges and potential changes, is able to figure out a way to overcome obstacles.	Recognizes challenges with some assistance, sometimes gets stymied by obstacles.
⬅			
Views failure as an opportunity	Welcomes mistakes as a necessary part of learning and is able to rise above them.	Is comfortable with mistakes as part of the learning process and mostly is able to rise above them.	Sees the basic connection between mistakes and learning, but not always able to rise above them.
⬅			
Draws from strengths and adapts around weaknesses	Recognizes strengths and weaknesses of self and others and is able to use these to an advantage.	Usually recognizes strengths and weaknesses of self and others, but is not always able to use this to an advantage.	Occasionally recognizes strengths and weaknesses of self and others, but is usually not able to use this to an advantage.
⬅			

    A teacher could use this rubric while he is circulating among the students and determine where each of them is on this spectrum. This would be like a snapshot of that particular day, showing where the student is at during the process. This rubric would be updated as the students continue to work and show progress until they have finally reached mastery. A completed version of this rubric might look like this:

Draws from strengths and adapts around weaknesses	Recognizes strengths and weaknesses of self and others and is able to use these to an advantage.	Usually recognizes strengths and weaknesses of self and others, but is not always able to use this to an advantage.	Occasionally recognizes strengths and weaknesses of self and others, but is usually not able to use this to an advantage.
	← 3/18	3/17 3/14	3/12

Once the student has reached the level of understanding, he would have achieved what is needed. He has demonstrated learning has taken place.

The challenges of using rubrics are that they can be difficult to create well. Relying on a program such as Rubistar is going to generate basic rubrics that do not really show what student achievement looks like. If you want a more detailed explanation as to why that is you can watch this YouTube video: https://youtu.be/DRZbNm0WrZc. In order to have one that best fits your students, most likely you are going to have to create it yourself. While creating it you will always want to use the mantra "what does this look like if students are demonstrating it?" If you keep that in mind, creating effective rubrics should be easy. Like anything though, once you try a few and get the hang of it, they will become even easier to create and use.

Power of observation

In today's day and age of SMART goals, or goals that are…

S – Specific
M – Measurable
A – Assignable
R – Realistic
T – Time-related

…we often minimalize the observational power of teachers. The thinking is that teachers are too subjective and this violates the "measurable" aspect. This also causes education to only value objective measures such as standardized tests, and as has been discussed previously, these do not necessarily measure the skills that we want them to. It is important not to devalue the importance the teacher plays in being able to determine whether a student gets it or not. Because we are with our students for 180 days of the year, we have the best seat in the house to observe their process of learning. Why should we not be part of the evaluation process rather than leaving it to an objective assessment? How can we factor in the experiences teachers have with their students? The simple answer is to make assessments that can capture the observations of teachers in a measurable and objective manner.

What this looks like can take many forms. It could be something as simple as the teacher taking notes on what she sees. It might look like this:

Research Day 5/13

- *Devon was seen gathering information from the National Geographic website. He spent a good amount of time looking over the information*
- *Keegan was sometimes on appropriate websites but other times was playing games or looking at Pokémon clipart*
- *Andrea was copying and pasting the information she was finding into the research document. Will have to check later to see that she puts this in her own words*
- *Jacob kept getting distracted by the students working next to him. Had to be redirected a couple of times but did find some interesting sites*

The teacher then could refer back to these notes to determine when each student achieved the mastery of researching.

However, notes like this could be difficult to sift through to determine student mastery. Another option to make things simpler is to use a graphic organizer that helps to keep track of student progress.

The teacher would use this one-page graphic organizer to monitor students and how well they perform certain tasks. Listed in the left-hand column are the tasks, the teacher records on which day(s) this task was performed, and then the teacher provides an evaluation of whether the student met, exceeded, or fell below expectations. The teacher could look at this sheet and come to the conclusion that Ben did a very good job on creating the poster, while Bonnie did not make sure the brochure was from the perspective of

Grading the Process ◆ 57

Goals	Major Tasks	Day 1	Day 2	Day 3	Day 4	Day 5	Day 6	Day 7	Day 8	Day 9	Day 10	Day 11	Day 12	Day 13	Day 14	Group member #1: Chad	Group member #2: Bonnie	Group member #3: Tracy	Group member #4: Ben	Group member #5
	Complete contract/set goals	X														X	X	X	X	
	Research colony of New Jersey		X	X	X											X	+	+	+	
	Synthesize the research in to bullet points					X													-	
	Create a rough draft of the brochure						X	X								+	X			
	Find maps/photos for use in the poster						X	X											X	
	Design a final draft on the computer of brochure								X	X	X	X	X			X	+	-		
	Get the posterboard								X	X								X		
	Print up photos/maps for use on poster										X	X	X			X			X	
	Create poster											X	X	X				X	+	
	Make sure poster from perspective of 1700s													X			-	X		
	Make sure brochure from perspective of 1700s													X		X	X			
	Use rubric to go over brochure														X	X				
	Use rubric to go over poster														X			X	X	
Goal #1: complete the project on time																				
Goal #2: get an A on the project																				
Goal #3: work together well																				

Project Deadline: January 25

+ = students exceed expectations
X = students meet expectations
- = students fall below expectations

the 1700s. This information could be used by the teacher to decide whether mastery was attained or not.

There are other examples a teacher could use; the key is finding one that matches your methods of observation. For instance, if you sit at your desk and observe student progress, you would be able to take the time to write detailed reports or make notes of certain skills that were displayed. However, if you are one that likes to move around the room, going from student to student while they are working, and recording your observations, then a graphic organizer might be a better way to do this. It gives you the flexibility of capturing a lot of information in just a small amount of space that can easily be referred to later.

Evaluating discussions

Discussions can happen at any point during the process of learning. The teacher might begin the lesson with a discussion to determine what students know about the topic. It might be used in the middle of the lesson to get students to consider something or think about it in a deeper manner. Discussions can also take place at the end of a lesson to figure out whether students understood the lesson and can use it in the context of something else. Lots of valuable information can be conveyed through these discussions, and depending on how students answer, the teacher will get a pretty good idea of their depth of understanding. Again, the challenge is capturing a discussion that can be fast-paced with lots of different people talking. How does a teacher keep track of what was said by whom and at what depth?

One suggestion would be to run a fishbowl discussion. What this involves is forming a circle of chairs facing each other in the middle of the room of up to a dozen seats. Then you invite whatever number of seats there are available to be filled by students. These will be the people taking part in the discussion. The rest of the class and yourself sit outside of the circle and observe the discussion as it is taking place, learning from what is being shared and debated.

This frees you up to make observations and note mastery by students. You may have to suggest questions to ignite the discussion, but for the most part, you are a non-participant. By doing this you will be able to pay close attention to the responses students are giving and evaluate how deeply the student is understanding them. You can take notes of your observations or use a graphic organizer to keep track.

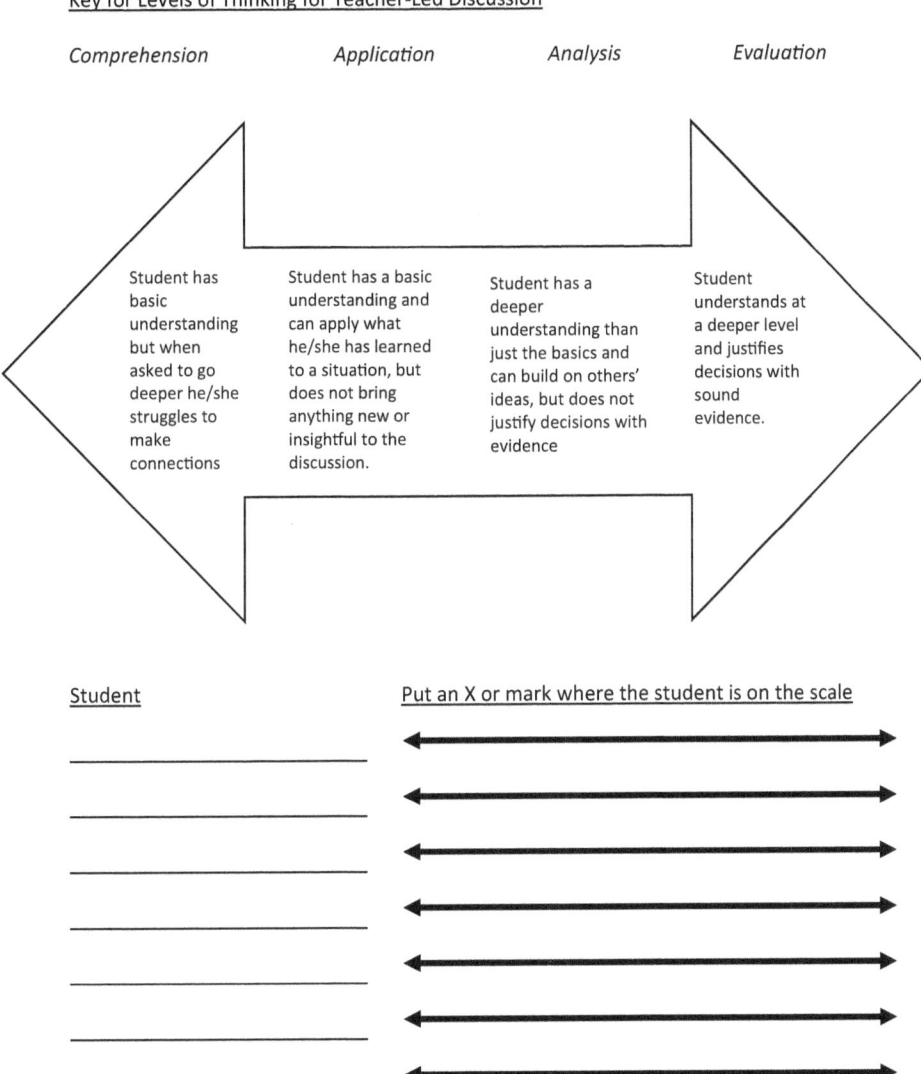

Another strategy is to have student-led discussions. What this might look like in a class of 30 students is you have six different discussion groups, each with five students. There are discussion starters for each group or you appoint a student moderator that is managing the discussion. Each group might be discussing the same points, or they might be doing something different, but by using this method, there are more chances for students to take part in the discussion, and it can go off in all sorts of interesting directions. One group might go really in-depth over a discussion starter while another may only talk about it at a surface level and move on to the next. You as the teacher are then circulating around the room, eavesdropping on these various conversations. When you hear something of depth and meaning, you can take note of that. The biggest drawback of using this method is that there is a pretty good chance you are not going to be able to catch everything that is said so you might miss something really insightful a student says. It can be tricky to juggle all of the various groups, but with practice, you will get better at it and be able to observe mastery from students.

A third idea would be to hold a town hall meeting. This involves having the entire class sitting in a circle. There is a moderator sitting in the circle or standing in the middle of it. This person does not lead the discussion so much as manages it. That means whenever the conversation begins to lag, this person throws something out there to ignite the discussion, keeping the fires of critical thinking burning bright. If the discussion is run properly, the students are generating the ideas and moving the conversation forward. This frees you up to observe the goings on and determining the students that seem to have gotten it, and those who still need some work.

There are ways to grade even if you are the one who is leading the discussion. A graphic organizer such as this would be a way to record not only student participation but the level of depth of student comments. (See the example on page 59.)

This scale uses Bloom's Taxonomy to allow the teacher to determine the level of thinking the student has demonstrated. If a student's responses are on the comprehension side of the scale, he might need some refinement or further study to gain a deeper understanding. If, however, a student consistently is on the right side of the scale, then you know she has achieved mastery and can now move on to something else.

Student reflection

Often, we task students with providing us with the answer. What if we flipped that on its head and allowed the student to ask the questions? Would that not be more meaningful to them and result in a deeper level of learning that is based on inquiry? In order to do this, we have to give students a space to explore such ponderings. Such a space exists in student reflection.

Student reflection can take many forms.

1. **Personal journal**: students will write a stream of consciousness about their experiences. These may be submitted occasionally to the teacher or kept as a reference to use at the end of the

experience when creating a more formal essay that reflects their experience.
2. **Double-entry journal**: students are asked to write one-page entries weekly. Students describe their personal thoughts, feelings, and reactions on the left page of the journal, while on the ride side they focus on key issues from class discussions or readings. Students then try to make connections by indicating relationships between their personal experiences and course content.
3. **Critical incident journal**: this purpose is to focus students on the analysis of a particular event that occurred during the week. Students are asked to consider their thoughts and reactions and explain how they might use this in the future
4. **Free association brainstorming**: this asks students to write down all the initial feelings they had when they first heard about what they were learning. After they finish, they share how these feelings have changed or strengthened throughout the process. Conclude by having them write about how they presently feel about it
5. **Quotes**: using quotes can be a useful way to spark reflection. Here is a quote as an example of what this might look like:

> If you always do what you've always done, you'll always be where you've always been.
> – T. D. Jakes.

You can use quotes from what you are currently reading or studying. Students can reflect on whether they agree or disagree with the quote or other thoughts and feelings that it incites in them.

6. **Reflective essays**: these are a more formal example of reflection. Prompts are provided and students write their thoughts on these. Reflective essays can focus on their own personal development, academic connections to the course content, or ideas and recommendations they might have.
7. **Directed readings**: students are given a reading or readings to look over and are then asked to reflect on what they think about it. This can eventually become the basis for class discussion.
8. **Structured reflection**: the following exercise is an example of a structured reflection discussion. List phrases that describe your senses/feelings. List phrases that describe your thoughts. What connections can you make between your own life and what we are learning about?

9. **"What if" reflection**: students will reflect on a what if scenario based on what the class is studying. This could be something such as how might things have been different if the Native Americans had repelled the invading Europeans? What if Hester Prynne had decided to reveal the identity of her baby's father in *The Scarlet Letter*? What if a polio vaccine had never been developed? And so on. This gets students to think about what they are learning in a different way.
10. **It's your thing/express yourself**: tell the students that they will have the opportunity to create their own version of their feelings toward what they are learning. Examples could include poetry, visual art (paintings, drawings, sculptures), music (rap is a rather popular choice for this exercise), individually created games or puzzles, or any form of creative outlet that gives the student the chance to perform or explain in front of the class. You will be amazed at the kind of creativity that surfaces in whatever way you do it.

Adapted from *Reflection Activities* By Diane Sloane. UMSL Center for Teaching and Learning: www.usf.edu/engagement/documents/s-l-reflection-activities.pdf

Student reflection typically is less formal than other forms of writing, but it also can do a better job of indicating to the teacher what the student truly learned. If you have created the proper environment, students will be willing to share honestly in their reflections and you will get a clearer picture of their level of mastery. Students can fake it in an essay. How many times have you yourself written an essay on a book you actually did not read and still managed to get a good grade? Reflections by their very name are a truer reflection of student achievement and will provide you with insight into the learning process of your students.

The nice thing about reflection is it can be used at any point during the process. You can get students' initial thoughts, gaining an understanding of what they already know. You can periodically collect their reflections during the learning process, trying to determine the moment that students show they understand what it is they are learning. It can even be used at the end if students have not shown mastery until this time. Different students will display mastery at different times, which means you will need to think about enrichment activities students can do once they have reached this understanding. As with all gifted students, this should not just be extra work but rather work that extends the thinking.

When evaluating a reflection, you can use a rubric. This is an example of one that determines the depth of the learning that has taken place (Kember, 2008):

1. **Habitual action** — At this level students look for material that answers the question. They paraphrase or summarize it, but without any real understanding. When asked, they cannot explain what they have written.

2. **Understanding** — There is an attempt to understand the topic or concept. Although students may search for underlying meaning, at this level, there is still no reflection. The concepts are understood as theory without being related to personal experiences or real-life applications. Students rely heavily on what the textbook or teacher has said. They will report that content accurately and with understanding but do not add any personal response to it.

3. **Reflection** — At this level, students not only have accurate understanding, they reflect on that understanding and are able to relate it to personal experiences, or they can make practical applications. If students are writing about experiences, those experiences will be considered and successfully discussed in relationship to what has been taught. There will be personal insights that go beyond theory.

4. **Critical reflection** — Implies the transformation of a perspective. Students start by recognizing their beliefs and accompanying assumptions. Something (new information, new experiences) disrupts that belief system, thereby forcing students to reconstruct or reform it.

The teacher would assign a 1, 2, 3, or 4 based upon the level and insight in the reflection, knowing that not many students are going to get to 4, but hoping most can get to 3.

Capturing conversations

One of the best ways to find out what students have learned is to have a one-on-one conversation with them. Students can guess on a multiple-choice, they can get by in an essay, but they cannot fake it talking about it with someone. The truth will come out. The challenging aspect of this method is finding the space and time to have these conversations with students. It requires different management of the classroom where the teacher is not the focal point but rather the bystander who is watching the students do the work. An example would be the teacher assigning a self-directed project where students are working independently, freeing up the teacher to move about the room and have conversations with individual students or groups. In these conversations, the students should be talking more than the teacher, but the teacher will use questions to generate conversation. Some of the conversation prompts might be:

- How are things going?
- What is something interesting you have come across so far?
- How do you think your progress is going? How could it be better?
- Do you agree or disagree with what we have been learning about?
- What do you think that would look like in the real world?
- Why do you think we should be learning about this?
- If you could change anything about it, what would it be and why?
- What do you hope to have learned when all is said and done?

The prompts could contain specific content about what students are supposed to be learning. The way students respond to these questions will provide you with a barometer of understanding. Recording where students are on this barometer will give you an idea of their level of understanding and can even determine mastery. You can record these conversations in many different ways. (An example can be seen on page 65.)

Notice that once an E appears, there is no need for further determining of the mastery because the student has shown a deep understanding of the lesson. Instead, the student can explore something related to this or move on to something completely different because he has already demonstrated mastery during the process. A graphic organizer such as this would allow the teacher to keep track of conversations and determine the level of understanding that students possess.

Student name	3/19	3/20	3/23	3/25	3/26	3/27	3/30	4/2
Jon	P	P	M	M	E	-	-	-
Logan	P	M	P	M	N/A	M	E	-
Minka	P	P	P	M	M	M	N/A	M
Krissy	L	L	P	P	P	P	M	M

E = student exceeds the expectation of understanding

M = student meets the expectation of understanding

P = student is progressing toward the expectation of understanding

L = student is limited in the expectation of understanding

N/A = did not have a conversation on that day

Portfolios

Portfolios are great because they act as a scrapbook of sorts for the process. The way a portfolio works is that students collect evidence that demonstrates they have mastered the lesson. This could be homework, reflections, exit tickets, quizzes, or printouts of online work – whatever they have produced that shows mastery. They are basically making a case for their learning.

Once the student believes she has reached mastery level, she turns in her portfolio to the teacher to determine whether this is the case. There are generally three types of student portfolios:

♦ Assessment portfolios: usually include specific pieces that students are required to know as displayed in quizzes, exit tickets, tests, and other forms of assessment, involving work that correlates with the curriculum.
♦ Working portfolios: includes whatever the student is working on, whether it be done in class or on his own. Can be less formal and more creative. May include mistakes and failures as these are part of the learning process.

- Display portfolios: this showcases the best work the student produces that is related to what the class is learning. It is a greatest hits that shows only the exemplars and not the mistakes that might have been made during the process.

How you decide to format the portfolio is completely up to you. You could have a very structured expectation of the portfolio with clear guidelines, or provide little structure, just asking that students collect work that acts as evidence of mastery. Here is an example of unstructured portfolio requirements:

> Collect five different pieces of your writing that you feel demonstrates your writing skills in this English-language arts class. Can be poetry, essay, short story, research notes, etc.

Students have free rein to determine what pieces best reflect their skills. This would be a route to go if you are teaching overall general skills such as writing, but if you are trying to narrow down what was learned to something more specific or tied to a content standard, you might want to be more specific with what you are looking for. Here is an example of a structured portfolio requirement:

> These documents must be included in appropriate sections:
>
> - Culminating project approved proposal
> - Completed time log
> - Final observation form
> - Written reflection: this two- to three-page essay elaborates on the content required by the rubric, a description of the project, an explanation of personal growth and new learning, and a description of challenges.
> - Artifacts: these items, along with the previous documents, offer proof that the student has learned.

Even though the requirements might be specific, there might not be a specific due date for the class to turn in the portfolio. Different students would be finishing at different times depending on whether they are able to produce the work that demonstrates their understanding. Then the teacher could use a rubric to evaluate the portfolio or the student might have to defend their portfolio orally to prove that she has achieved mastery much like a doctoral candidate would. A rubric for such a portfolio presentation might look like the example on page 67.

The great thing about portfolios is that much like a scrapbook, students can look back, using them to see how far they have come in the process. This might mean reviewing a concept they are struggling with, it might act as a

Grading the Process ◆ 67

Overall	Defense of Portfolio	Portfolio	Reflection
Excellent	• Presents in a professional manner, speaking clearly and confidently throughout. • Makes a clear case for the progress that has been made over the course of the semester, using lots of evidence to make the point. • Is able to answer any questions that are asked with meaningful answers that show reflection of the work.	• Has chosen 5 or more examples of work that clearly shows the progress of the student over the semester. • Portfolio is well organized and easy to find things with a table of contents and/or tabs.	• Shows an understanding of what was learned at a deeper level, not just content. • Has identified strengths and weaknesses and ways to improve these. • Has a clear plan moving forward on how to use what was learned in future work.
Good	• Presents in a professional manner, speaking clearly and confidently but not consistently throughout. • Makes a case for the progress that has been made over the course of the semester, but could use more evidence to make the point. • Is able to answer most questions but not always meaningful answers that show reflection of the work.	• Has chosen 3 or 4 examples of work that shows the progress of the student over the semester. • Portfolio is organized with a table of contents and/or tabs, but not always easy to find things.	• Shows an understanding of what was learned but is not introspective, just content. • Has identified strengths and weaknesses but not ways to improve these. • Has an idea moving forward on how to use what was learned in future work but no clear plan.
Needs Improvement	• Does not present in a professional manner, either not speaking clearly and/or confidently. • Does not make a case from the progress that has been made over the course of the semester, lacks evidence. • Is not able to answer most questions or answers do not show an understanding of learning.	• Has chosen 2 or fewer examples of work that shows the progress of the student over the semester. • Portfolio is not organized, lacking a table of contents and/or tabs making it difficult to find things.	• Does not show an understanding of what was learned, misses the boat. • Has not identified strengths and/or weaknesses. • Does not have an idea moving forward on how to use what was learned in future work.

reference to help them solve a problem that involves that concept, or it might just be a confidence boost to remind them of the successes they have had.

Self and peer evaluations

These are an excellent way of determining mastery during the process. For the teacher to consider himself the only set of expert eyes in the classroom would be a missed opportunity. There are 30 or so other experts in the classroom as well that can determine whether a student has gotten it or not. Your students might even have a better perspective than you because they are privy to their inner-thoughts in their self-evaluation and conversations the teacher is not a part of in the peer evaluations. Students are the ones smack dab in the middle of the process so who better to determine what sort of mastery has been achieved?

Because you are trying to capture understanding during the process, the self and peer evaluations should be done throughout, not just at the end as a summative. The best way to do this is to take snapshots every couple of days or so. You could use a graphic organizer such as this:

Part of the Lesson	Peer _____	Peer _____	Peer _____
Research			
Creation of Product			
Lesson Prep./ Presentation			

You can see that this self and peer evaluation has broken the learning down into parts, the first part of the process being the collection of research, then the creation of the product, and finally the lesson preparation and presentation of what was learned. These various snapshots will give you an overall picture of what students are learning during the process. It also breaks it down by skills should you need to do that for grading purposes. A completed peer evaluation might look something like this:

	Peer - John
Research	5/1 A – he came up with about five pages of notes from internet research
	5/2 B – started out getting research but got distracted by a friend near the end of the period
	5/3 absent
	5/4 A – brought in a book he got from the library on photosynthesis. He also helped to organize the group's notes
Creation of Product	5/7 B – contributed notes to the PowerPoint but worried more about the sound effects than the content of the slides
	5/8 C – I saw him on YouTube watching silly videos instead of finding visuals. Did finally locate a good visual on cellulose breakdown
	5/9 D – while other watched the PowerPoint and offered suggestions, he was on his phone
Lesson Prep./ Presentation	5/10 C – did not take much of a leadership role and presented only on 2 slides out of 20
	5/11 B – did offer some good feedback on how demonstration can go better but argued with Anthony a lot on his part

John was evaluated by a group member nine times during the process of learning, with varying results. The teacher could look at this and determine that when he gets to work independently, John tends to do better as evidenced by the As and Bs during the research process. However, when the process turned to collaboration during the creation of product, John seemed to struggle, as reflected by his B, C, and D. John could certainly be given credit for having mastered the skill of research but would still have some improvement to make when working with others.

One thing you will need to make sure to do is set clear criteria so that self and peer evaluations are consistent from student to student. From the example before, do all students in the class know what A work looks like, or the difference between B and C work? You will know the criteria were not clear if when you get the evaluations back, there is a large discrepancy between various students grading the same person. In other words, if Jeff has been evaluated by three groupmates, resulting in him receiving an A, B–, and D, how could three people be seeing such a difference in Jeff's work? Were the criteria clearly explained to students so the expectations were consistent? Here is a rubric with an example of clear criteria:

Part of the Lesson	Self Ronnie	Peer Bobby	Peer Ricky
Research	3 - I found a bunch of research on volcanos but could've found more	4 - Showed us where some great websites were & found the most information	2 - Researched some but was also playing on-line games
Preparation	2 - I wasn't too helpful during this part but gave a few ideas	4 - Had the idea for how to display the volcano & built most of it	4 - Came up with the materials & helped to organize notes
Exhibit	3 - Typed up some of the info. sheets but misspelled a couple of terms	4 - Typed up most of the info. sheets for the board & printed photos	3 - Helped to design the tri-fold but forgot to bring in border

| 1 – Does not contribute to the group, actually holds it back. | 2 – Does little to contribute to the group but occasionally helps. | 3 – Contributes to the group in a positive manner and helps to make it better. | 4 – Contributes mightily to the group, leading by example and making it better. |

At the bottom, what a 1, 2, 3, or 4 stands for has been clearly laid out. Students have also been instructed to justify their rating by showing what this looks like. If a student received a 4 and the comment is simply "did great work," the logical question would be what does great work look like. However, if there is a description that shows what this excellent looks like such as the 4's that Bobby received, "Had the idea for how to display the volcano and built most of it," the teacher can get a much better idea of whether the student is mastering the learning.

The self and peer evaluations merely act as additional information the teacher has access to in order to determine student mastery. Why would you not want to tap into this resource and take advantage of the expertise of your students by making them a part of grading the process?

Do we have a problem here?

Ultimately the big question is how does all of this grading of the process translate into a letter grade that both demonstrates the mastery the student possesses in PrBL as well as meets the expectations that the school system has for grades? Because it looks different than your typical classroom, your gradebook is going to look different as well. You have to think about grading from an entirely new perspective, although you might arrive at the same summative grade that most school systems require teachers to produce. For instance, students might not all have the same number of grades. It might take student A three grades to demonstrate mastery while student B did not achieve this until seven grades had been recorded. It is the collection of these mastery grades that will make up the final grade that appears on the report card.

We put all sorts of resources into our toolboxes in order to make us effective teachers. Everyone knows there is not a single way to do almost anything, and having options and choices is going to better allow you to match up the evaluation with the skills you need to grade. This is why creating an appropriate assessment toolbox is going to help you in grading the process. By using a couple or many of the suggested assessments, you will be able to keep track of the learning process your students undertake. This is going to require you to think about grading a little differently and to get good at hitting a moving target, but just like anything, the more you practice it, the better you will become.

Activity #5

Look at how you do assessments right now. Are they mostly formative or are they summative? If you have formative assessments, can these be turned into methods of grading the process? How could you modify those for that purpose? How can you create additional assessments that can be used throughout the process to determine mastery not just at the end, but while the learning is occurring? Create rubrics or means of measuring these assessments.

6

Keeping it Real

Authentic Learning

> ### Problem #6
> *You know that the best sort of learning for students is experiential learning where they are actually getting to do what it is they might be doing in the real world. How do you know this? Because you were a student-teacher and you know all of the theoretical learning that you did in the college classroom before becoming a student-teacher really did not do you much good. It was the experience itself, working with real students, creating real lesson plans, and problem solving real classroom situations. This is where you learned the most because it was authentic. You want your students to be able to have this valuable experiential learning as well, but you are confined within the four walls of your classroom.*
>
> **Learning objectives:**
> - How do you bring the real world to your students?
> - What does authentic learning look like?
> - How can you make the learning students do in your classroom more authentic?

The good news is that by simply engaging in problem-based learning with your students, you are instantly making the learning more authentic. But like most things, just doing the action is not enough to make it so. You have to do the activity with fidelity. What is meant by this? It is like being at the gym and going through the motions of working out. You get on the treadmill for a

DOI: 10.4324/9781003302605-7

few minutes, lift some barbells that are not too straining, and work up a mild sweat. But not really pushing your limits or having a plan for how you are going to do it will not get the results you are hoping for.

It is the same for a problem-based learning classroom. Having students go through the steps and work on a problem without attaching it to the real world and making it authentic is not going to provide the experience you want for your students. If you are having students work on PrBL but they still are working on math problems that have no connection to their lives, developing identical products as others, or writing essays that are seen by no one but you, then you are not really being authentic. The logical question is, what does it mean to be authentic?

What does authentic learning mean?

In its most basic definition, authentic learning is real-life learning. It is more complex than that of course, but for the most part, these two go hand and hand. Although there are many different ways to achieve authentic learning, the elements for these methods must contain most if not all of the following qualities:

1. Are ill-defined, requiring students to define tasks and subtasks needed to complete the activity
2. Comprise complex tasks to be investigated by students over a sustained period of time
3. Provide the opportunity for students to examine the task from different perspectives, using a variety of resources
4. Allow competing solutions and diversity of outcomes
5. Create polished products valuable in their own right rather than as a preparation for something else
6. Provide the opportunity to collaborate
7. Are seamlessly integrated with assessment
8. Can be integrated and applied across different subject areas and lead beyond domain-specific contents
9. Provide the opportunity to reflect
10. Have real-world relevance (Reeves et al. 2002)

Numbers one through six are taken care of by the structure of PrBL. Having a big hairy problem with multiple ways to approach and solve is extremely authentic because that is the way most problems present themselves in real life. If you are grading the process, as was discussed in Chapter 5, then you are doing number seven. The more comfortable you get with PrBL, the more willing you might be to co-teach across multiple subject areas because, again, this is how things will occur in the real world. It is not like you are at work and a bell rings and you are doing math. Then another bell rings and you are now switching to ELA. The subject areas typically mush themselves together in the working world. You might be an accountant focused mostly on math, but there are aspects of ELA and economics that you will have to have in order to do your job well. You might be an engineer where you are using both math and science to solve problems. As a social studies or science teacher, you have to use ELA to communicate lessons to students and math to determine grades. Creating cross-curricular problems will allow students to see how a problem might require several aspects of learning in order to solve it.

Reflection is an additional assessment that you might use formatively or summatively, which is designed to bolster learning. If done correctly, students will learn how to reflect on their own and lead to improvements in the future. People who are able to do this tend to have an easier time with their adult life than those who do not because by learning from their mistakes, they become better workers, better spouses, better parents, and better human beings in general. Reflection is a natural step of the learning process and because it is integrated into the PrBL, it is not its own step but something that permeates through the DNA of the work. How to intentionally do this with students will be discussed further in Chapter 8.

We have covered the first nine qualities of authentic learning, but how do you ensure your PrBL has real-world relevance? How do you create experiences where students are making connections to the real world and finding the learning relevant to their lives? You can work to make the three elements of PrBL authentic, which are:

1. Problem
2. Product
3. Audience

Making just one of these aspects authentic is a step in the right direction, but to make sure your problem-based learning is done with fidelity, you should try as much as possible to make sure you have hit all three of these.

Making the problem itself authentic

There are various ways to do this, from using actual real-life situations to creating simulations that mimic real life. However, just creating a word problem that seems to take place in real life would not be authentic if it is not relevant to the students themselves. Take this problem for example:

> Angelica is making herself a dress. She needs 2 yards of red fabric, 1.5 yards of green, and 0.75 of white. The red fabric costs $3.95 per yard, red costs $4.50, and white is $6.00. If she buys just enough fabric to make the dress, how much will she need to spend?

Certainly, a real-world problem as people use fabric to make dresses and it is figuring out cost, which people have to do all of the time. However, how many of your students do you think make their own dresses? So why should they care about such a problem? How is it relevant to their lives? In order to make the problem authentic, you need to center it around something that students actually care about.

A better problem using the same concepts would look like this:

> Angelica is buying candy. She needs 0.5 pounds of M&Ms, 0.75 pounds of jellybeans, and 1.25 pounds of gumballs. The M&Ms cost $13.95 per pound, jellybeans $7.50 a pound, and gumballs are $9.00. How much will she need to spend to get all of the candy she needs?

While not everyone makes their own dress, most children, no matter what the age, like candy. It is something they would be buying for themselves possibly and something they would want to buy. There would certainly be more excitement and motivation to buy candy rather than fabric. Of course, we do not want to assume this necessarily. There are ways to figure out what your students care and do not care about.

You can capture student interests by doing student interest surveys with your classes. One might look like this:

STUDENT INTEREST SURVEY

1. My favorite subject is…
2. These are three specific topics I like about this subject…
3. The three things I do best at school are…
4. The three things I do best in my free time are…
5. My favorite sport or game is…
6. I would like to get better at…

7. I would really like to learn about…
8. When I grow up, I would be interested in…
9. A goal I have set for myself this year would be…
10. When I go on YouTube, I like to watch videos about these three things…

If you were designing it for younger children, it might look like this:

Circle the emoji that shows how you feel about each statement

1. I like school ☺ 😐 ☹
2. I like to write ☺ 😐 ☹
3. I like to solve problems ☺ 😐 ☹
4. I like to draw and do crafts ☺ 😐 ☹
5. I like to do things with my hands ☺ 😐 ☹

And this could go on and on, depending on what information you want to glean from students that would inform the topics of your problems. You might even want to use an interest survey as a pre-assessment to see what students know about the topic the lesson will cover and what they would be interested in learning more about.

EGYPTIAN INTEREST SURVEY

Use a scale of 1–5, 1 being no interest, 5 being high interest

1. How interested are you in mummies?
2. How interested are you in pharaohs?
3. How interested are you in pyramids?

> 4. How interested are you in Egyptian mathematics?
> 5. How interested are you in the various kingdoms (Old, Middle, New)?
> 6. How interested are you in hieroglyphics?
> 7. How interested are you in the Nile?
> 8. How interested are you in Egyptian religion?
> 9. How interested are you in Egyptian medicine?
> 10. Overall, how interested are you in learning about the Egyptians?
>
> Is there anything else you are interested in learning about the Egyptians that was not mentioned here?

Although some of these topics might not be relevant to skills they will need in their regular lives, it is relevant to their interests. You could use a survey such as this to craft a problem focusing on the aspects that students showed the most interest in.

It could be something that students do not know about but could come to care about because it is a universal and timeless concept. They may not know who Oliver Brown is, but once they investigate it and discover that this was a father fighting for the right of his black daughter to go to the school of her choice, they will begin to care because it is centered around issues that they do care about: equity and discrimination, which are issues that still plague us today. They might know very little about who Jonas Salk is, but once they research his development of the polio vaccine and how many lives it saved, not to mention how he did not seek to patent the vaccine so that it could be used globally more economically, they might see the relevance in the recent development of the COVID-19 vaccine and how drug companies did seek to make profit from it. Because students care about themes within the topic, the problem becomes more relevant and thus more authentic.

Making the product authentic

What does it mean by authentic product? The product is meant to act as a summative assessment. It brings all of the work students have been doing into one place where there should be a demonstration of mastery. Of course, if you have been grading the process all along, this product should be of no surprise to you. You know what students have been doing, you know what they are understanding, and you know what level of mastery they already are at. Regardless, often in the real world, we do have to bring all of this learning into a final product.

What should these products look like if they are to be authentic? According to Jon Mueller, an authentic product should be one "in which students are asked to perform real-world tasks that demonstrate meaningful application of essential knowledge and skills." The key words to pull out of this definition are:

- Perform real-world tasks
- Demonstrate meaningful application
- Essential knowledge and skills

As mentioned before, project-based learning focuses greatly on the product while problem-based learning looks at the process to get to the product. Nonetheless, there is a product that students must create to show what they have learned. This product can take all sorts of forms and can even be determined by the students. No matter what the product, it should be something that looks like something people would have to create in the real world. Very few people in the real world write an analysis of the book they have been reading. Your boss is probably never going to give you a set of math problems to figure out. And no one in the real world takes a multiple-choice test. Most of the products created in the real world are performance assessments. Some of these might include the following:

- Oral presentation – often, you will have to present an idea or the work you have been doing to colleagues or a superior. Being able to do so with confidence, persuasiveness, and clarity is going to make you more successful in your work, so being able to do so with a certain amount of skill is going to give you an advantage.
- Debate/speech – similar to an oral presentation, you will work with people who you do not agree with or who are trying to advance their own agenda over your own. You need to be able to argue with them civilly because doing so in an uncivil manner could result in getting fired. Debate and speech allow students to learn how to disagree while maintaining professionalism.
- Role playing – although in the real world you are not role playing the part of someone else, it is important to be able to see multiple sides and perspectives on an issue. Role playing is an excellent way for students to learn this. Students might also be role playing the part of

a job they wish to have in the future such as assuming the role of a lawyer in a mock trial or the role of a businessperson.

- Group discussion – a lot of work involves synergizing with colleagues and creating a plan so that everyone is rowing the row in the same direction. There is back and forth on this, ideas are shared, and points are made. Being able to successfully get your voice heard in a group discussion as well as taking what others have shared to create something new are important skills to take into the workplace.
- Interview – being able to conduct an interview will help you on both sides of the interview because 1) you will know how to ask questions to get what you want to learn from someone, and 2) it helps you see how professional people answer questions in an interview. If you are interviewing a university professor about the effects of global warming as part of your final product, you are going to be exposed to someone who does this for a living and you will be seeing an exemplar that you yourself can model.
- Portfolio – this is a collection of student work with their reflection. This has two important aspects to it. First, a portfolio is something that will be useful for students to learn how to create because often in college or when trying to get a new job, employers want to see your body of work and what you have accomplished in the past. This acts as a sort of expanded resumé where you can show off the work you have done as well as showing potential employers what you are capable of. Second, the reflection aspect helps students to become self-learners. In other words, students are often waiting for the teacher to correct them or note what could be improved. We want students that can self-correct and understand for themselves how they can make their work better. Ultimately, we want to be creating life-long learners who are self-directed in making their work better. The reflection aspect can help with that.
- Exhibition – this is merely a physical representation of student work. Traditional exhibitions might be a trifold, a slide deck, a poster, a model, or other created work. The key to an exhibition is, much like an exhibition at an art museum, it needs to explain everything without you actually being able to explain it verbally. In other words, an artist is not standing by his work explaining to you what he did. Instead, there is a placard that explains the work of art, a video that shows its creation, or some other means of communicating what was meant. A really good exhibition should stand on its own with enough details that it does not need to be explained.
- Essay – although students might not ever have to submit the traditional, five-paragraph essay to their place of employment, they

probably will have to communicate through writing. The purpose of an essay is to be able to express in written words a case for why your idea makes sense. An essay does a good job of teaching the basics of this with its format, call for detail, use of transition sentences, and inclusion of evidence. There are many different ways to submit writing in the workplace, either through a briefing, a review of a product, a summary of work, a recommendation, or other sorts of writing (Stanley, 2014).

These can be used to make products that take the form of products students would create in their lives, making them real world. These are products that students will see again once they are out in the workforce, thus they demonstrate meaningful application. They also contain essential knowledge and skills. You will notice in this list of assessments that students will have to use many of the 21st-century skills sought by employers discussed in Chapter 2:

- Analyzing thinking
- Active learning
- Collaboration
- Complex problem solving
- Critical thinking
- Creativity
- Leadership
- Resilience
- Technology use

These are all skills students will be learning throughout the process of problem-based learning. As a result, the PrBL product becomes very authentic because these will be skills that are used later on in life.

Finding an authentic audience

Students often do assignments that no one but the teacher is going to see. It is seen by one set of eyes, graded, and then handed back. It could be made authentic by having the product presented to a person or persons outside of the class who are either experts on the topic or who have an interest in the topic.

For example, students could write a legal brief if the problem has something to do with the law and send this to a practicing lawyer to assess. Or letters to members of Congress can be written that can make the argument of lessening the amount of coal we use or a request to consider the way we fund schools. For math, what if students used their skills to solve a real-world problem and then give it to the very person who would be concerned with such a problem. If you are teaching perimeter and area, have students tackle the problem of designing a new obstacle course for the local park. They have to design the park and choose all the obstacles contained within it but also have to pay attention to the perimeter and area to make sure it fits in a spot that the park has available. Once this is complete, it can be sent to city council, the parks and recreation department, or the city planner to see if such an idea would be a good one. In social studies, students write resolutions for how they would solve a problem in another country and then present this in a room with hundreds of other students from around the area doing the same thing. Or maybe they develop a business plan and present it to a panel a la Shark Tank, made up of local businesspeople. In science, students can develop an invention, design a plan, create a model, and then present it to judges. Maybe students develop a plan for helping to maintain an ecosystem, going out to the location, and coming up with ways to protect it, the audience being the animals, plants, and organisms that get to continue to grow as a result.

Here is a scaffolding of various authentic audiences you might find for your students:

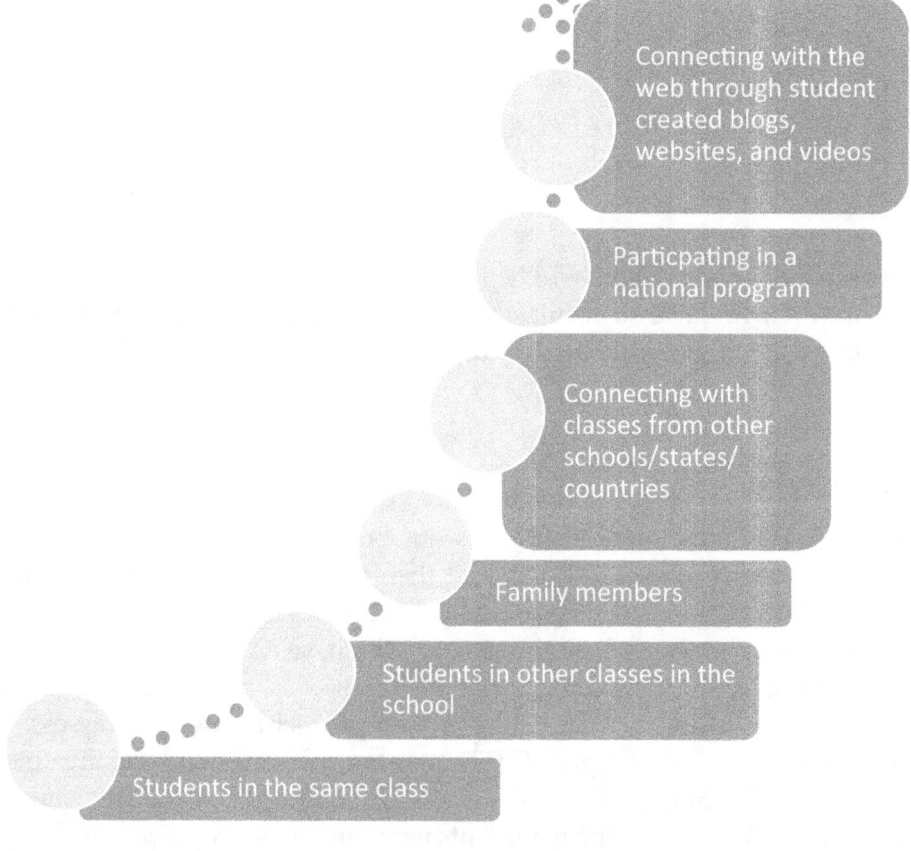

In addition, you can ask experts to weigh in on student work and evaluate it with an eye to what they see in their everyday jobs. Some experts you could consider would be:

Math	ELA	Science	Social studies	Arts
• Architects • Engineers • Financial planners • Mathematicians • Statisticians	• Authors • Critics • Editors • Journalists • Technical writers	• Biologists • College professors • Doctors • Ecologists • Researchers	• Businesspeople • Economists • Historians • Lawyers • Politicians	• Actors • Artists • Film directors • Graphic designers • Musicians

There are authentic audiences everywhere, you just have to figure out how to connect them to your class. With the availability of Zoom or Google Meet, it is more easier to connect to audiences than ever because they do not have to leave their home or place of business in order to give you some of their time.

Do we have a problem here?

Using the problem-based learning structure is not enough to make a lesson authentic. There are other things you have to do as the teacher to help make it relevant to students and thus meaningful to learn. You can do this by making...

- ♦ Problems
- ♦ Products
- ♦ Audiences

...more authentic by connecting them to the real world as much as possible. It is important not just to assume what is relevant or should be relevant to students. Gathering information through surveys and conversations will give you an idea of what is relevant to student lives.

To help you in making your PrBL more authentic, there is a matrix in the appendix that allows you to pick authentic problems, products, and audiences from columns to make your lesson more grounded in the real world.

Activity #6

If you have started to create a PrBL lesson, go through it and make sure you have met all of these guidelines:

- *Are ill-defined, requiring students to define tasks and subtasks needed to complete the activity*
- *Comprise complex tasks to be investigated by students over a sustained period of time*
- *Provide the opportunity for students to examine the task from different perspectives, using a variety of resources*
- *Allow competing solutions and diversity of outcomes*
- *Create polished products valuable in their own right rather than as a preparation for something else*
- *Provide the opportunity to collaborate*
- *Are seamlessly integrated with assessment*
- *Can be integrated and applied across different subject areas and lead beyond domain-specific contents*
- *Provide the opportunity to reflect*
- *Have real-world relevance*

Are there any that you are missing? Are there any that could be done with more fidelity? Where are some opportunities for you to make the lesson more authentic?

7

Raising the Rigor

Problem #7

There are a lot of gifted and high achieving students in your class and you have been tasked by your principal to make your class more challenging. Unfortunately, your principal has not given you any specific ideas for how to do this. He simply states, "it needs to be more rigorous."

Learning objectives:

- ★ What is rigor? What is it not?
- ★ How do you increase it in your classroom?
- ★ How can you make sure there is rigor in your problem-based learning lessons?

What is rigor? It's the million-dollar question because like other teaching terms such as differentiation, personalized learning, and growth mindset, we throw them around like they are the band-aid designed to fix all classroom problems. And truthfully, these terms can be used to great success in the classroom but the problem is a lot of teachers actually do not have a great understanding of what they are, what they look like, or how to use them in their own classroom because they have not been given the proper training. Rigor certainly falls under that category.

DOI: 10.4324/9781003302605-8

What rigor is and is not

If you were to check a thesaurus for the word rigor, a couple of synonyms that would be found would be "difficult" and "hard." This might be accurate in some instances, but in the context of the classroom, these terms are not synonyms. There is a clear distinction between difficult and hard as compared with rigor, but many educators don't understand this. They are told to add rigor to their class and they think it means to either make the work really hard, or even worse, to give more of it. These are not what rigor is.

For example, a teacher without an understanding in an effort to add more rigor to an assessment might ask questions that are more obscure or not as commonly known. Take this science question for example:

> If the sky is dark blue, does this indicate that the sky has more or less pollution than a sky that is light blue?

Appears to be a rigorous question, but it is really not. You either know that a dark blue sky indicates a lack of pollution and a light blue means it is the result of air pollution either in the form of coal burning or chemical power plants. You would know this from having read it somewhere, heard it spoken by a teacher, or seen it on a program or video. Using logic or thinking skills would most likely result in the incorrect answer because one would assume the sky would be darker when polluted but this is not the case. It is a difficult and tricky question, but it is not a rigorous one because when it is all boiled down, the answer is dependent upon remembering something that was told to you.

Here is another question that might be mistaken for rigorous when in fact it is merely hard:

$$6 \div 2\,(1+2) =$$

Using logic, you start with the parenthesis first and get 3. You multiply the 2 by the 3 still in the parenthesis and get 6. Then you complete the question by dividing 6 by 6 which equals 1, correct? Wrong. This is the way equations used to be solved. Now there is what is known as PEMDAS which stands for:

P = parenthesis
E = exponent
M/D = multiplication/division
A/S = addition/subtraction

Starting with the parenthesis you would divide 6 by 2 and get 3. Because multiplication and division are done in the same order, you start left to right, meaning you divide 6 by 2 and get 3 as well. To complete the problem, you do what remains and you multiply 3 times 3, getting 9. Seemingly a rigorous question but that too is not correct. If you have memorized the PEMDAS formula you simply follow it step by step. None of the math is terribly difficult so you would easily arrive at your answer of 9. There is no critical thinking taking place here, just the application of the formula.

If neither of these questions is rigorous, just how do you raise the rigor? It is really simple; you get students to think at a higher level. How do you know what a higher level means? Wouldn't it be different depending on the person and their ability to think? Is that not subjective? Actually, it is not. Higher-level thinking can be categorized by using Bloom's Taxonomy, which breaks it down like this (Francis, 2016, 2021):

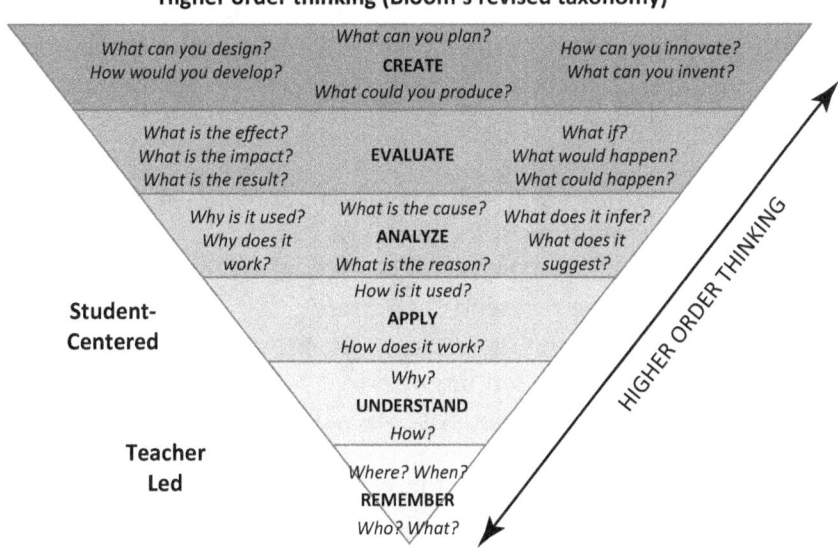

It starts with the bottom half of remember, understand, and apply. These are lower-level questions that access content knowledge and may even go so far as to ask students to utilize it in a situation, but there is little critical thinking taking place. Students either heard it, comprehended it, or followed its steps to arrive at an answer. Even looking at the questions on the figure, it asks where, when, who, what, how, and why, but all of those questions result in a single correct answer. Because of SMART goals and our desire to make assessments as objective as possible, we as teachers ask a lot of lower-level questions on our assessments:

ELA: Find the parts of speech in the sentence. (apply)
Math: Solve these problems. (apply)
Social studies: Who was the first man on the moon? (remember)
Science: How does gravity work? (understand)

If one were to try to add rigor by making the questions harder, it might look like this:

ELA: Find the parts of speech in the sentence. Then find the phrases and clauses.
Math: Solve these problems. Now solve more of these types of problems only with bigger numbers and more steps.
Social studies: Who was the first man on the moon? Who was the second?
Science: How does gravity work? How does gravity on Mars work?

The questions are definitely more difficult, but students are still using the same thinking skills in order to solve them. If you are going to add rigor, you need to ask questions from the upper half of Bloom's pyramid: analyze, evaluate, and create.

ELA: Find the parts of speech in the sentence. Replace the adverbs in order to change the overall tone of the sentence. (create)
Math: Solve these problems. How might you see problems like this present themselves in the real world? (analyze)
Social studies: Who was the first man on the moon? From 1969 to 1972 there were six moon landings and yet we haven't been back for over 50 years. Why do you suppose we haven't had the motivation to do so? (evaluate)
Science: How does gravity work? What if gravity did not work as it does? How would that affect our planet? (evaluate/create)

Now we're doing some thinking.

If you have done some analysis of your own while reading through this section, you probably noticed the major difference between the lower- and higher-level questions is the number of possible correct answers. For the lower-level questions, there is typically only a single answer that would be considered correct. Sure, this can be improved or made worse by the use of detail or showing your work or not, but it all comes back to that single correct answer. The higher-level questions on the other hand could have many possible answers. Thirty students could give 30 different answers and yet they could all be correct. For this question…

ELA: Find the parts of speech in the sentence. Replace the adverbs in order to change the overall tone of the sentence.

...some students could change the adverbs to make the tone sad, while others might make the sentence more positive with their choice of adverbs. There might be two students who make the tone sad but use different adverbs. There are endless correct possibilities.

How to make your PrBL rigorous

Now that you know the difference between hard and rigor, the question becomes just how do you create problem-based learning lessons that are rigorous? It all starts with an ill-defined, open-ended, essential question. What this does is open both sides of the problem to make sure students will have to be doing some sort of higher-level thinking in order to work on the lesson.

Why is it important to be ill-defined? Students are used to being led step by step through what they are supposed to do in class. This certainly creates students who can follow directions, but it does not create independent thinkers. You want to make the question a bit cloudy, where everything is not clearly laid out on what is supposed to occur. It is actually the lack of focus on the problem that forces students to have to find it themselves. It requires the students to have to define tasks and even subtasks in order for them to work on the problem.

Here is an example of an ill-defined problem:

Prisoners sentenced to life in prison should have the option of choosing death.

There are many undefined aspects to this question:

- Prisoners from where?
- What are the circumstances of their life in prison situation?
- What would their options be?
- How soon would this be carried out after choosing death?
- Who will carry out the sentence?
- What are the ramifications for countries or states that do not have the death penalty?

Students would want to develop as many of these questions as possible, and then either answer them for themselves or research and find situations that might help in defining the aspects more clearly. For many of these, there is no right or wrong answer. There is merely the answer supported by the strongest evidence found or the clearest argument they want to make.

This does not mean the problem will remain ill-structured for the duration. It is up to the students to complete these tasks in a manner that they determine for themselves in order to come to a clear solution, and there is always a structure to follow.

Making the problem open-ended means not putting a ceiling on what can be learned. A PrBL is not set up correctly if students ever get to a point where they feel they are done. If you ask students to work on a lesson with a single correct answer, once they have found the answer, they have completed the lesson. This is why having open-ended problems with multiple solutions, each of those solutions being able to go in many different directions, will give your students enough to do to never be finished. This does not mean students cannot come to their own conclusion and find evidence to make their points and be ready to defend their position. It means that if students were to get to that point and had time left, they would have the option to explore other possibilities, perspectives, and situations. The rule of thumb for students partaking in PrBL is that they never finish their problem, they just run out of time to explore anything more.

This is why giving students a deadline and a softly structured schedule will be helpful to students who have difficulty managing their time. The structure of PrBL gives students checkpoints and an idea of when tasks need to be ready. You might give students two weeks to work on a problem, providing them with a pacing calendar that looks like this:

Day 1	Day 2	Day 3	Day 4	Day 5
Discuss the problem with your group and take out the important aspects	Develop your essential question/problem statement	What questions do you need to address in solving this problem?	Research problem/questions	Research problem/questions
Day 6	Day 7	Day 8	Day 9	Day 10
Develop solution	Develop solution	Finalize your solution	Practice your presentation of your solution	Present your solution

This is a pacing calendar because students do not need to be exactly where it says they should be. It may take more than a day to develop their essential question/problem statement, they may only need a single day to research, and developing the solution may only take a couple of days or might carry over into the practice day. Regardless, this gives students an idea of where they should be and if they are not, they can adjust accordingly. The only thing that stays consistent on the pacing calendar is the due date of when the solution will be presented, but this too is subject to change. If students are working hard in their groups and it appears an additional day or two would lead to an improvement on the final product, then days may be added at the discretion of the teacher. If students appear to be getting work done at a faster pace, it probably would be better to help them find ways to dig deeper and make the product better rather than making it due at an earlier date.

Big hairy problems are a great way to ensure that the problem is open-ended because big hairy problems can rarely ever be completely solved. For example, if you had this big hairy problem:

How do we make our cafeteria food healthier and more nutritional?

Throwing a couple of celery sticks and carrots onto the menu is not going to be an easy fix. There are numerous things to consider such as even if you do make healthy offerings, how do you get reluctant students to eat them? Or do you remove unhealthy options such as French fries even though by doing so you will be diminishing the profits of the cafeteria? This is a problem hundreds and thousands of schools have sought to tackle, using all sorts of various strategies, but it is an ever-changing solution and once one aspect of the issue is solved, another one pops up in its place. This is what causes it to be open-ended and allows students to explore even deeper because there is no definitive answer.

Finally, to ensure that your PrBL lesson is rigorous, you or the students need to write a problem statement in the form of an essential question. The essential question you might have right now of course is just what is an essential question? The key is in the word essential. This is what you or students hope to uncover by the time they are finished working on the lesson. What can you point to in order to determine that students did indeed master what you asked them to or asked of themselves?

Grant Wiggins and Jay McTighe list the characteristics of a good essential question in their book *Essential Questions: Opening Doors to Student Understanding*:

1. Essential questions are open-ended and don't have a single, final, and correct answer.
2. Essential questions are thought-provoking and intellectually engaging. They also promote discussion and debate.
3. Essential questions call for higher-order thinking, such as analysis, inference, evaluation, and prediction. They can't be effectively answered by recall alone.

4. Essential questions point toward important, transferable ideas within disciplines.
5. Essential questions raise additional questions and spark further inquiry.
6. Essential questions require support and justification, not just an answer.
7. Essential questions recur over time. They can *and should* be revisited again and again.

Let us put these four essential questions to the test and determine whether they fit the bill for the characteristics mentioned above.

- What was the United States' response to Pearl Harbor?
- How can we reduce the effects of global warming?
- Why might we go to war with North Korea?
- What problems and solutions are presented by strip mining?
- What was the United States' response to Pearl Harbor?
  This would not be a good essential question because it is not very open-ended. This is a question a student could look up in a history book or even ask Alexa and get a pretty serviceable response. Plus, it does not require any higher-level thinking. This is an understanding or recalling question. It could easily be turned into a good essential question by rephrasing it as "Was the dropping of the atomic bomb on Japan justified by what happened at Pearl Harbor?" All of a sudden this becomes an argument rather than a presentation of facts. Students could make cases for either side and in order to justify their position, a higher-level thinking verb, they will have to present the same facts they would have had to in the original question.
- How can we reduce the effects of global warming?
  This would be a good essential question because it is very debatable, making it open-ended. There is more than one way to reduce global warming and there are varying opinions on which ones are the most effective. There are even those who would claim that global warming is a myth. It also would require research and justification to support any solutions that are developed.
- Why might we go to war with North Korea?
  Even though this is a why question, it is not a strong essential question. It is true, it could be debated or there may be several reasons, but the major issue here is that this is not really a problem. The question requires students to make a case for why we might go to war with North Korea, but it is not giving them the room to solve a

problem. With just a few changes though this could be changed into a better essential question. "How can we prevent going to war with North Korea?" With this change, now it is a problem just waiting to be solved. Now students have to determine not just why we might go to war with North Korea, but what can be done to avoid this.

- What problems and solutions are presented by strip mining?

    This is a good essential question because it is debatable, it is thought-provoking, a bit controversial, and it will raise all sorts of additional questions such as what other science is controversial. It is also written in a way that does not indicate which side is more correct than the other. If it had read… "what solutions does strip mining present and why might someone be opposed to it" …it is clearly leading the students to the solutions being the correct side of the argument. You want students to make this decision for themselves so phrasing it this way allows students to weigh both sides and then come up with their own decision.

In the writing of your essential question(s), you want to make sure to use the upper levels of Bloom's in order to challenge the thinking of students.

It continues in your day-to-day questioning

Rigor should be provided not just in the development of the essential question, but it should permeate the class and be part of its culture. This means students seeing and hearing higher-level questions all of the time rather than periodically. Here are places higher-level questioning can be used in the classroom in addition to PrBL:

- Homework
- Worksheets
- Labs/hands-on assignments
- Discussion
- Writing prompts
- Projects
- Reflections
- Assessments

This means having an awareness of the types of questions you are asking. Are they higher level, do they require a different kind of thinking, do they have multiple possible answers? A lot of times we think we are asking higher-level questions when in fact we are not. A good rule of thumb is to look at the verb in the question. It typically provides a clue as to what level the question is being asked.

Here is a list of the verbs and the level of thinking they are typically associated with:

Bloom's Key Verbs

Remembering	choose, define, find, how, identify, label, list, locate, name, omit, recall, recognize, select, show, spell, tell, what, when, where, which, who, why
Understanding	add, compare, describe, distinguish, explain, express, extend, illustrate, outline, paraphrase, relate, rephrase, summarize, translate, understand
Applying	answer, apply, build, choose, conduct, construct, demonstrate, develop, experiment with, illustrate, interview, make use of, model, organize, plan, presents, produce, respond, solve
Analyzing	analyze, assumption, categorize, classify, compare and contrast, conclusion, deduce, discover, dissect, distinguish, edit, examine, explain, function, infer, inspect, motive, reason, test for, validate
Evaluating	appraise, assess, award, conclude, criticize, debate, defend, determine, disprove, evaluate, give opinion, interpret, justify, judge, influence, prioritize, prove, recommend, support, verify
Creating	build, change, combine, compile, compose, construct, create, design, develop, discuss, estimate, formulate, hypothesize, imagine, integrate, invent, make up, modify, originate, organize, plan, predict, propose, rearrange, revise, suppose, theorize

This means being purposeful about using these verbs when asking questions either in written or verbal form to ensure there is rigor in the work. There are several ways you can do this:

- Phrasing: teacher communicates the question so that the students understand the response expectation (i.e., no one-word answers).
- Adaptation: teacher adapts the question being asked to fit the language and ability level of the students.
- Sequencing: teacher asks the questions in a patterned order indicating a purposeful questioning strategy, going from lower Bloom's to higher.
- Balance: teacher asks both lower- and higher-level questions and balances the time between the two types. The teacher uses questions at an appropriate level or levels to achieve the objectives of the lesson.
- Participation: teacher uses questions to stimulate a wide range of student participation, encouraging responses from volunteering and non-volunteering students, and redirects initially asked questions to other students.

- Probing: teacher probes initial student answers, and encourages students to complete, clarify, expand or support their answers.
- Wait time (think time): teacher pauses three to five seconds after asking a question to allow students time to think. The teacher also pauses after students' initial responses to questions in class.
- Student questions: teacher requires students to generate questions of their own.

Creating this culture of higher-level questioning in your classroom is only going to work if you ask higher-level questions in nearly everything that you do rather than just sporadically.

Pushing students into Domain D

In order to marry the higher-level questioning you are using in your classroom to the relevance of the learning, you can use Domain D of the Rigor/Relevance Framework developed by the staff of the International Center for Leadership in Education. Domain D is a combination of getting to higher levels of thinking such as analysis, synthesis (creating), and evaluation that PrBL allows for students, but doing so while applying the problem to a real-world situation. The Center defines it as follows:

> Students have the competence to think in complex ways and also apply knowledge and skills they have acquired. Even when confronted with perplexing unknowns, students are able to use extensive knowledge and skill to create solutions and take action that further develops their skills and knowledge.
>
> (Jones, 2004, 4)

Here are some of the examples of lessons the Center gives for what Domain D might look like using PrBL:

Language arts:
- Simulate a presidential debate.
- Write a legal brief defending a school policy.
- Prepare a demonstration video (Jones, 2004, 8).

Mathematics:
- Create formulas to predict changes in stock market values.
- Design support posts of different materials and sizes to handle stress loads in a building.
- Develop a sampling plan for a public opinion poll (Jones, 2004, 9).

Science:
- Explore designs of car safety restraints using eggs in model cars.
- Design and construct a robot.
- Discuss the social, ethical, and emotional consequences of genetic testing (Jones, 2004, 10).

Social studies:
- Analyze a local, state, or national issue and prescribe a response that promotes public interest or general welfare (e.g., a voter registration campaign).
- Research and debate economic issues and public policy related to the Internet, such as sharing online music.
- Analyze a school/community problem, suggest a solution, and prepare a plan to solve it (Jones, 2004, 11).

All of these are asking students to solve a problem that manifests itself in the real world. Notice the verbs used in these problem statements – they are almost all on the higher end of Bloom's, meaning that while students are trying to solve these real-world problems, they are also having to think a bit more. It has pushed the lesson into Domain D where the students are going to see *why* this is important and *how* they can develop a solution using higher-order thinking.

Do we have a problem here?

In order to raise the rigor of your classroom, you need to be asking the right questions, and more importantly, they need to challenge the thinking of your students. By designing your questions using Bloom's Taxonomy, and being cognizant of what types of thinking students will be engaged in, that is what you will be doing.

When you create your essential question:

- Determine how many essential questions you will need
- Frame your questions in "kid-friendly" language. Make them engaging and thought-provoking
- Write essential questions with "how" or "why" instead of "what"
- Sequence your questions so they lead naturally from one to another
- Post these questions in your room as a learning focus for your students
- Remember - If a question is too specific, or could be answered with a few words or a sentence, they are probably not essential questions (Wiggins, 2007)

Activity #7

Go through your assignments and see how many higher-level questions you are asking. You can use a chart such as this:

Ques.	CS	MC	SA	ER	GR	Lower Level Ques.			Higher Level Ques.		
						Remb.	Under.	Appl.	Anal.	Eval.	Creat.
1.											
2.											
3.											
4.											
5.											
6.											
7.											
8.											
9.											
10.											
11.											
12.											
13.											
14.											
15.											

After seeing your distribution of higher-level questions, ask yourself if there is something more you could be doing to raise the rigor in your classroom.

Also consider when you are verbally asking questions. What is your distribution for that? You can use a chart such as this to keep track of that as well:

Level of Bloom's	How many times it is being asked
Remembering	
Understanding	
Applying	
Analyzing	
Evaluating	
Creating	

The only way to raise the rigor in your classroom is to be aware of the levels of thinking you are asking of students. You should gather data to make the determination as to whether you are where you want to be.

8

The Power of Reflection

Problem #8

You have done your level best to teach your students what they are supposed to be learning, but there can sometimes be a divide between what you want your students to learn and what they actually learn. You might have intended them to learn how to write a literary analysis while they may have learned how to put an assignment off until the last minute and still turn in serviceable work. How do you get these two things to mesh?

Learning objectives:

★ How do you discover what it is students actually learned from a lesson?
★ How can you use this information to plan future lessons?
★ How do you marry your intended learning with their actual learning for the best learning possible?

Think of reflection as a supplement that you take in order to make the learning even stronger. It is essentially learning about the learning. This helps students to better determine the why of what they learned and how it will be useful for them. This personalization is what really matters to students.

DOI: 10.4324/9781003302605-9

The advantages of using reflection

As you have already learned, PrBL is all about process and experience. This is a very powerful way to learn and leads to a more enduring understanding. It is the difference between students learning it long enough to take the test, and students being able to access it years after leaving your classroom in order to better their lives. It is the experience that makes it stick. However, as educational pioneer John Dewey once said, "We do not learn from experience. We learn from reflecting on the experience." This reflection is where the true learning takes place. If you don't know what it is you actually learned, it is hard to take that lesson and move forward with it. If, however, you are able to reflect and figure that out, that is when the light bulb goes off, where the connection is made, and how the learning becomes ingrained.

What exactly does reflection do for students? If done properly, reflection can:

- Offer context to students
- Check in on personal goals
- See how they felt about the lesson and what was learned
- Allow them to process what occurred
- Help them to see the lesson in steps
- Provide awareness for their own work management
- Celebrate what worked
- Fix what didn't
- Give them space to work through the emotions experienced through the process
- Assign a space for feedback to the teacher

Most importantly, reflection continues to give students a voice in their own learning. Just as you have provided students with lots of autonomy throughout the PrBL process, reflection is the perfect way to cap off the lesson. Students get to determine what they learned and what they didn't. The grade does not determine that for them.

How to reflect

We use the word reflect a lot but just what does it mean? When we reflect, we think about something that we might not otherwise have given much thought to. To reflect means really breaking down and thinking about the experiences, actions, feelings, and responses throughout the lesson, then interpreting or analyzing them in order to learn from them (Atkins and Murphy, 1994; Boud et al., 1994). The best way to do this is to ask ourselves questions about what we did, how we did it, and what we learned from doing it. Students might not come to these questions very naturally because they might not have been asked them before. This is a new type of learning for them, and like any form of new learning, you have to expose them to it, provide them with exemplars, and model for them how it works.

An example would look like this:

Now that we have finished the unit on poetry, reflect upon the following:

- What was something you thought you did well and why?
- What was something you wish you had done better and why?
- What was the most important thing you learned about the topic, yourself, or your classmates?
- How do you see yourself using these skills in your own life either presently or in the future?
- Do you think it was worthwhile learning about poetry? Explain your reasoning.

These questions are designed to get students to think a little deeper about the work they have just completed. Notice they are not yes or no questions, or if they are, they ask students to explain why. This could be done as an exit ticket, it could be assigned as homework, or it could be something they turn and talk to another classmate about. But questions such as these guide the students and give them a track with which to follow. Without it, students might have difficulty asking those challenging questions or be willing to dig a little deeper, or they might go completely off track. Starting students in the process of reflection with guiding questions can help to build their capacity to do so on their own after they have seen it done a few times.

You also want to create an expectation of what responses should look like. You have to change the mindset of students who often approach questions in school as items that just need to be answered. They need to show not tell what was learned: 2+2=4 is telling you the answer, but are you showing it? How did you arrive at four for the answer, what strategy did you employ, and what process did you follow? We often save the phrase 'show your work' for math class, but it really applies to all learning. Show us the process you went through while doing the learning and share your feelings and thoughts about that experience.

You also want students to be honest and forthcoming with their responses. What you don't want is students giving you the answer they think you want from them. It is important not to attach a grade to assignments such as this. You do however want to provide feedback on their reflections. Not feedback such as you use too many run-on sentences or there could be more details used. The feedback is a conversation you have with the student that asks that essential question of what you wanted them to learn and what they actually learned. You can learn a lot about your student by talking about this as well as your practice of teaching.

It might be a good idea the first time you are conducting a reflection that you make it a class discussion rather than a writing assignment. You use the questions posed before and ask them in a classroom setting. By doing this, you can control the quality of the responses with follow-up questions. For example, if you ask:

- What was something you wish you had done better and why?

And the student simply mutters that he wishes he had received a better grade – you can break this down and ask follow-up questions such as:

- What grade were you trying for?
- What do you think prevented you from achieving that grade?
- What could you have done differently to get that grade?
- What does that look like?
- How did this make you feel?
- Why do you suppose you didn't do those things necessary to get your desired grade?
- If you could travel back in time and give yourself some advice before this lesson began, what would you tell yourself?
- Why is the grade so important to you?

These follow-up questions are designed to pull the details out and show the sort of responses you are looking for.

Another way you can handle this is to reflect upon the lesson from your point of view about your own role in the lesson. Questions you might want to address:

- Did the lesson go as I hoped it would? What evidence do I have for my answer?
- Once we got into the lesson, what did I realize I needed to add to make it better?
- What do I believe went well with the lesson?
- What do I think is my biggest failure or regret in this lesson?
- What would I change about the lesson for next year?

You must be sure to provide detailed answers, use examples, and at times, be vulnerable. For example, in answering this question:

- What do I think is my biggest failure or regret in this lesson?

Your answer might look something like this:

- One thing that I failed to do in this lesson was to provide the rubric to students before they began to work on their final product. I waited until the last minute rather than doing it before I introduced the lesson. This would have helped to focus students a little more and given them guidance on what they should be striving toward. It also would have focused my teaching a little better as I would have known what goal I was trying to steer students toward. I'm a bit frustrated with myself because I knew that I needed to get it done but just kept putting it off and then once I did it, it was rushed and not of the best quality. I could have even created the rubric with the class so that they had a voice in it and could see how it was set up for easier understanding.

This response models for students the sort of response you would like to see from them. It is detailed, has several examples, and admits that things could have been better had you been more responsible. It is an honest assessment of how the lesson went and students can see for themselves that you are not looking for a clean, canned answer but rather how things really went and what was actually learned. That's the point of a reflection.

Creating a culture of reflection in the classroom

By modeling reflection at the beginning of the school year, you are starting to form a culture of reflection in your classroom. The best way to continue this is simply to make sure students are reflecting as much as possible and in many different ways. This means it needs to be purposeful until the moment comes where it doesn't need to be. Once students have got the hang of it, you can remove the prompts, and then the students are naturally arriving at these questions on their own.

It should be part of the natural PrBL cycle:

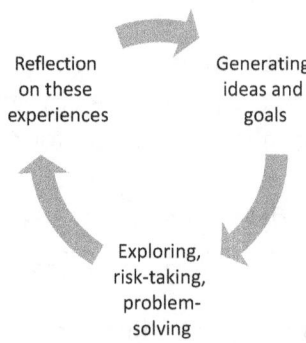

Just like a routine of when to line up or what the procedures are for turning in homework, students will know that a reflection is coming at the end of every problem-based learning lesson because you are always asking them to do one. It is part of the experience of PrBL and students know they will always have a voice in the learning process.

Notice how the cycle does not stop once you get to reflection. What has been learned carries over to the next lesson and can be used to make it better. If a student were to reflect that they should have spent more time revising their final product, what will hopefully happen is when they are in the middle of the next problem, they remember this and make sure to allow for plenty of time to revise the final product and end up producing something better.

Although reflection should be routine in the PrBL classroom, it should not feel like a routine. What is meant by this is if you ask the same five prompts at the end of every lesson, students will become tired of these and probably begin to groan when you pull them out after yet another lesson. Part of the culture you create should be varying the types of reflection that you use. The remainder of this chapter will give you several options for switching it up a bit yet keeping the consistency of asking students to think about their learning.

Scaffolding the thinking for students

The critical thinking model contains sequenced questions that move you, step-by-step, through a thinking process:

- How did the product turn out? (Descriptive)
- What was your role in creating it? (Descriptive)
- What did you learn in the lesson? (Descriptive)
- How do you feel about the end result of the lesson? (Analytical/reflective)
- Was there anything that could have been done differently to improve the results? (Analytical/reflective)
- Do you think you learned everything you wanted to? (Analytical/reflective)
- If you could change something about the lesson, what would you choose and why would it make things better? (Reflective/evaluative)
- What could you change about yourself to get the results that you want? (Reflective/evaluative)
- Where can you go from here in future lessons using PrBL? (Reflective/evaluative)

First students are encouraged to be descriptive, then analytical, and finally evaluative. Each part of this process is important, but taken together, it provides a framework for questioning that constitutes reflection. The scaffolding of the questions takes students who think at a surface level and pushes them to dig in a bit more. If they follow the progression, they should be doing actual reflection on their practices and toward improvement.

Different protocols

There are many different protocols that can be used in order for students to be reflective of what they learned. However, most of them follow the steps of the Gibbs Reflective Cycle.

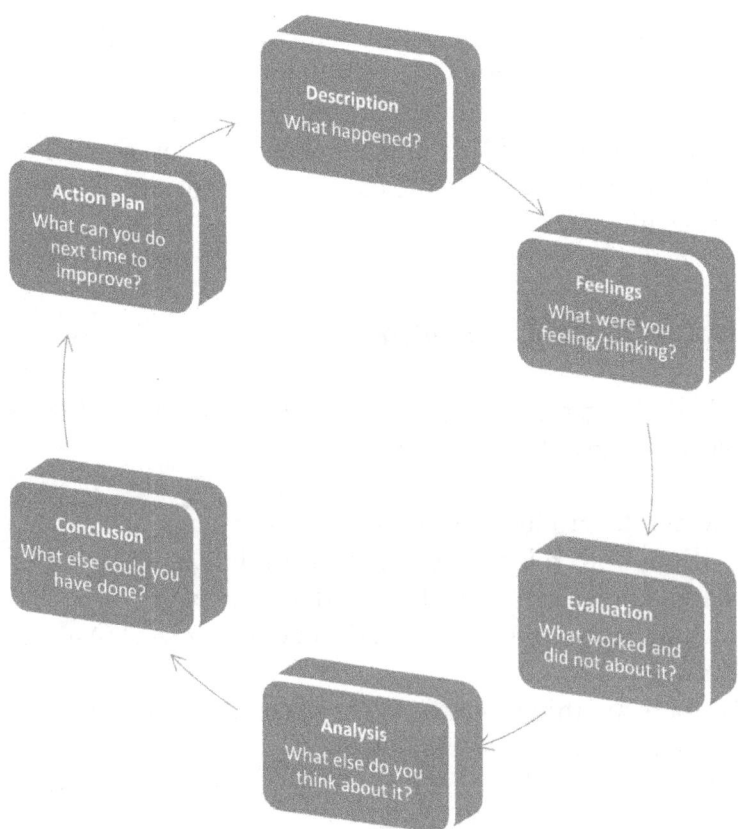

Whichever protocol you decide to use with students, it needs to have the space to allow students to consider all of these. One of the most basic protocols you can use with students that does an effective job of allowing students to reflect properly is known as a SWOT analysis:

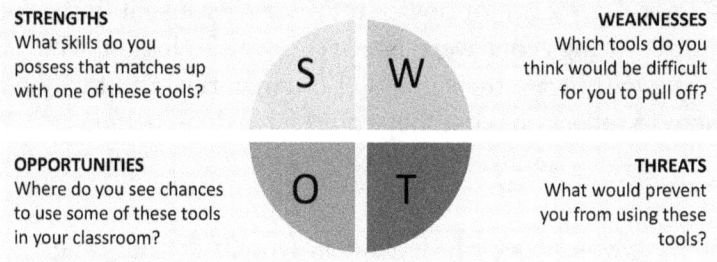

The SWOT analysis looks at four areas of the work:

1. Strengths
2. Weaknesses
3. Opportunities
4. Threats

By answering these questions, students will get a complete picture of what they did well and not so well in the past, and how they can improve upon this in the future.

You could have students answer this on a piece of paper, they could have conversations with fellow classmates, an interview with the teacher, or some other creative outlet. It is a fairly basic protocol that checks all of the boxes for what students should think about concerning what was learned.

If you are looking for reflections that are a bit more creative, here are five different protocols you may consider using with students that will mix things up:

1. 3-2-1
2. Snapshot
3. Twitter
4. Video confessional
5. Letter to a Student in Next Year's Class

The 3-2-1 protocol looks like this:

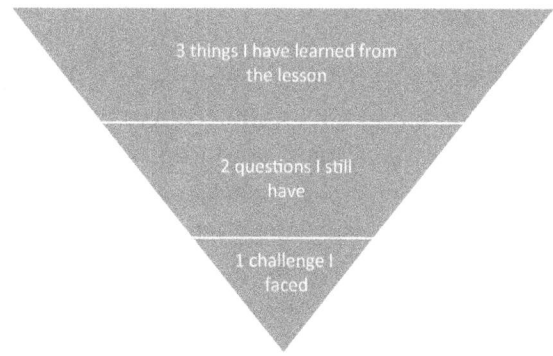

This is a good protocol for novice reflectors because it first asks students to just list three things that were learned from the lesson. The 'two' questions are going to indicate their grasp of the material, and the one challenge requires them to reflect on what they could have done better.

Example:

1. Jane Eyre was a pretty independent woman for her time
2. Charlotte Bronte could write a really good romantic comedy
3. You should marry for love, not convenience

1. Would the book have been as effective if it were told in the third person rather than from Jane's perspective?
2. With the book being written in 1847, does it still have lessons for those in the 21st century?

1. Not waiting until the last minute to get the reading in. Instead of reading 100 pages in a day, maybe if I read 25 a day over the course of the week, I would enjoy it better

The snapshot protocol is good to use with students who have been working in a group together. It is a reflection of the success of the collaboration as much as it is what content was learned. What it asks students to do is to create five snapshots. These snapshots are like a still life with students frozen in a position that conveys their thoughts and feelings:

- Snapshot #1. What was the most important thing that was learned by the group from the lesson?
- Snapshot #2. When things were going well, what did it look like?
- Snapshot #3. When things were not going well, what did it look like?
- Snapshot #4. Do a selfie that conveys what you think your individual contribution to the group was.
- Snapshot #5. The next time you are working in a group, what would you want it to look like?

Students are not supposed to explain anything or talk. Then the class tries to interpret what their snapshot says with the group explaining afterward how accurate the interpretation was. This is a good protocol to use with students in order to get them moving as well as able to express their creativity. To take this to the next level, you can even take snapshots of the snapshot on your phone to show students later in the year so they can determine whether they have indeed improved in their collaboration.

The Twitter protocol forces students to reflect in a very concise manner. Here are the constraints of the protocol:

- What is something you learned today either about yourself or in general? (Cannot be any longer than 140 characters)
- Have an accompanying picture/meme that sums up your feelings
- Add a hashtag to it as well that shows what you are going to improve for next time

Examples:

Thought I knew a lot about biodiversity but think again
    #managetimebetter
Research papers aren't that hard if you follow the outline
    #readytotryusingAPA

This protocol should be used with more experienced reflectors because it asks students to go to the analysis and reflection phases of the process very quickly. It also gives you a finger on the pulse for how students are feeling with the use of the meme. You should be able to determine whether any reteaching needs to take place or if they might be ready to move on to something more challenging. The hashtag gives you something to look for the next time they are working on something similar.

The video confessional is like the sequence in a reality show where the camera is on a single person and they express their thoughts and feelings about what went on. In this case, the student would share their thoughts and feelings about the lesson. These can be done on a video program such as WeVideo, Flip Grid, or whichever one replaces these once they become obsolete.

You could provide guiding questions such as the following:

- Describe the lesson in a sentence or two
- What big idea did the lesson help you to understand?
- What do you feel was the most important thing you learned from the lesson?
- What do you wish you had spent more time on?
- Where do you think you did your best work?
- What was the most enjoyable part of the lesson?
- What was the least enjoyable part of the lesson?
- What could the teacher do to make the lesson better next time?

Or if you feel students have a good understanding of what it means to reflect, you could just allow them to do a stream of consciousness where they talk about whatever they want concerning the lesson. You might want to give them a time constraint to help them focus some of their thoughts.

A video confessional allows for a few things:

- Students who might not be strong writers but who can explain themselves fairly well will have their voices heard more clearly
- It allows the teacher to see the emotions and feelings of the students
- It allows the students to see their own emotions and feelings, which might surprise them on playback and create more self-awareness
- It makes a record of student progress that they can watch later and compare with other such reflections
- It makes for a much more entertaining assessment than traditional reflections
- Gives you the opportunity to offer video feedback of your own

The final protocol is called Letter to a Student in Next Year's Class. In this, students are writing a letter to someone who will be taking the same class next year, answering these three basic questions:

- What should they learn from the lesson and how they should go about doing this?
- What mistakes did you make that you want to warn them about so that they do not repeat them?
- What should they know about the teacher in order to be successful in the class?

It might look something like this:

Dear Student in 2024,

I am writing this letter to you to let you know about the unit on geography. For this lesson, you will be looking at the problem of where the city should put a rec center that would benefit the entire community. You have to consider several things about it concerning geography including where there is available land, what is the terrain of the land available, and where the population centers of our town are located.

At first, I thought this was really obvious; just put the center in the middle of town and that way no one is having to travel too far to get to it. The problem with that though is that there is not much available land in the middle of town for the size of structure you have planned to build. In addition, the middle of town is very flat and part of your plan is to create walking and bike trails that provide exercise for people. Walking or riding on flat trails does not give them much of a challenge. My biggest piece of advice is to find geographically a space that allows for expansion of the rec center but does not make it too far for some people. You also have to consider where most of the residential areas are and where people will be coming from.

By this time you have probably worked on a few problem-based learning lessons. If you were like me, you might find these annoying because Mrs. Kidwell makes you do all the work and it just seems like she is walking around the room talking with kids. You especially might not like the fact that she likes to talk about her cats all the time (I'm a dog person). Just enjoy the fact that you are not being talked at or made to do stupid worksheets. At least with these you are getting more choice in what you have to learn so take advantage of that and choose things you really care about.

Sincerely,

Robin

A reflection such as this requires students to not only think about the lesson as it stands today, but how they might look upon it once a year is passed. Hopefully, this will get them to think about the long-term effects of the learning and how it might benefit them later. It will help them to gain a perspective on what they did.

There are many more ways that you can have students reflect. If you are looking for ideas, you can go to www.thegiftedguy.com/resources where there is a section containing several other reflection protocols to consider.

Do we have a problem here?

If you want to get the most out of problem-based learning, the process is more than just the learning. It is learning from that learning and the best way to do this is through reflection. Reflection might come easy to some students but it might not for others. You need to put things into place in your classroom that support the reflection of students. One of the biggest gifts you can give concerning this is the gift of time. Taking an entire class to reflect the day after a product has been turned in will create a culture in your classroom where reflection is simply the expectation. You might feel as though this time could be better spent with students learning something new, but the question you have to ask yourself is once you teach them something new, if they forget it right away, isn't that an even larger waste of time? By using reflection, you stand a much better chance of students having an enduring understanding of the lesson and using what they have learned in the future.

> **Activity #8**
>
> *Although you have probably been doing this throughout reading this book, you might have been doing so internally. Take this opportunity to put your thoughts to paper, going through one of the reflection protocols and reflect on how PrBL might change your teaching practices, what you are scared of in implementing it, and your next steps. Then after trying PrBL for a few lessons, look back at this reflection and see if your thoughts have changed. Look back a year from now. Two years. Use this reflection as a marker to the start of your journey using PrBL.*

9
The Role of the Teacher

Problem #9

You find yourself teaching in a problem-based learning classroom, things are running pretty smoothly, but you have one big problem – what are you supposed to do now? Whereas before you were finding and giving students information in a variety of ways, now students are doing this for themselves. Instead of giving assessments or worksheets, students are determining for themselves whether they understand it or not. Rather than you asking questions of students, they are asking their own. You find yourself having to do none of the usual things a teacher has to do, so what do you do? Catch up on emails, organize your desk drawers, or finally watch that Netflix series you've been meaning to? You have to find something to do that will enable your students to learn better than they are already learning. But what does that look like?

Learning objectives:

- ★ What does your role as the teacher look like in a PrBL classroom?
- ★ How will you manage your time and space to be able to observe the process of learning as it is taking place?
- ★ How will you help to push students beyond the basics and encourage them to go a little deeper to where the real learning lurks?

DOI: 10.4324/9781003302605-10

Because problem-based learning is not the traditional way of teaching, methods typically associated with this way of teaching are not going to be as effective. You need to change your mindset about the role of the teacher in a PrBL classroom. Instead of being the disseminator of information, you are the motivator, to take the information that students find for themselves and use it to its greatest effectiveness. Part of this is getting students to think beyond the obvious – help them to arrive at those ah-ha moments, and encourage them to think more critically. Of course, this is always easier said than done.

How can you push students to think critically?

The good news is that you have been establishing a culture of thinking in your classroom already. By having students raise the rigor as was talked about in Chapter 7, they will be aware of what higher-level questions sound and look like. They have used these skills to write essential questions for their PrBL that will enable them to learn the lesson at a deeper level. And you have followed this up by asking higher-level questions in your day-to-day interactions with students so they are exposed to them consistently.

Ultimately though what you want to happen in your classroom is that students ask these questions themselves, not just in the essential question, but at every juncture of the process. Asking questions that are going to allow students to dig deeper is going to be important, especially when they are breaking the problem down and trying to figure out how to approach it. Your major role as the teacher in a PrBL classroom is to help your students recognize when these moments come and encourage them to use these skills to raise the rigor themselves. This can happen in a multitude of ways but there are three main areas where you can have a large impact. These are:

- Student conferencing
- Meddler in the middle
- Cognitive tasks analysis

Student conferencing

Conferencing is talking with students one-on-one or in groups depending on if they are collaborating with others, which they will most likely be in PrBL. Because of the independent structure of PrBL, this frees you up from the front of the classroom and allows you the time to sit down and have conversations with your students. Part of the goal of these conversations should be learning more about your students, but they should also be about finding out what they are doing and challenging them to go deeper in their studies. You generally have three different purposes for student conferences:

1. Status conference
2. Process conference
3. Reflecting conference

Status conferences involve checking in with the student or group to make sure they are where they need to be in regard to the progress toward their deadline. The main purpose of these types of conferences is to see how students are doing in balancing their time management. You or the group has likely created a pacing calendar and you want to check to make sure they are not getting too far behind. You sit down with the group with this calendar in front of them and see the progress of their area of responsibility. You might find some group members either right where they need to be or ahead of the pace, while others seem to be falling behind. You can have further conversations with these struggling students, but allow those whose progress is going as planned to work independently. What you don't want is to get to the end of the lesson and come to find some of the students haven't been doing much or got stuck on something and they have no product to offer. These conferences can often be about compliance.

Status conferences need not be too formal. It could just be a checking in with the group already knowing how they are doing because you have been observing them as you walk around your classroom, grading the process. In some cases, the only thing you will need to do is to provide encouragement. Other times it might be more involved, especially if there are issues that need to be resolved. Even though you are the teacher, it is important to let students have productive struggles. That is where a lot of the learning takes place so you shouldn't be too quick to offer up a solution, but rather let them figure it out for themselves or offer a strategy. At the same time, there will be moments where you will have to step in as the adult of record and offer advice or do some mediation. Use your professional judgment to determine which is needed but always err on the side of giving students space to get themselves out of their own mess.

Although you are constantly making status checks with groups as you move about the room, monitoring the progress of their work, it might be a good idea to schedule at least one formal status conference a week, preferably in the middle of the week. This is so if students are struggling and you have not caught it yet, you can address it before they get too far behind and get them back on track.

Process conferences, as their name implies, are about looking at the process of problem-based learning. It is checking each step along the way to make sure students are pushing themselves further by asking higher-level questions. These process conferences do require the teacher to use more probing questions, which will enable deeper digging than the status ones. Here you are checking to make sure what students are producing is going to be valuable for their problem. Ideally at each step of PrBL, you are touching base with them to ensure the depth of learning. Here are some questions you might consider:

1) Present the problem – have they considered all perspectives with the problem rather than going to the most obvious perspective?
2) List what is known – is there anything missing or anything that could be explored further? If not, rather than giving them the answer, suggest they analyze certain ones.
3) Develop a problem statement – have they written an essential question(s) that is open-ended and that uses the upper levels of Bloom's?
4) List what is needed/ask questions – is there anything missing or are there additional questions that need to be asked? Again, don't give them those questions but use inquiry to guide them there.
5) List actions, solutions, or hypotheses – does their solution ask them to analyze, evaluate, and/or create?
6) Present and support the solution – have they considered their audience and how they are best going to convey what was learned?

You don't have to meet with groups for every step of the process. Some of these questions might be addressed through written feedback. There might be checkpoints such as having students who are spending the week conducting research, turning in their notes that were taken for the teacher to look over, and returning with comments meant to push them.

Reflection conferences can come at any time in the process. They are often done at the end of the lesson, although they do not have to be. As mentioned in Chapter 8, the questions asked here are trying to get students to get below the surface and determine what it was they truly learned from the lesson. Although protocols can be used to help them to reflect, just sitting down with the teacher and reviewing how things went can be a valuable form of reflection, especially if students are just learning how to reflect. The probing questions the teacher might ask will help them to understand what it means to reflect deeply.

It can be even more effective once you have evaluated their product and can go over the rubric with them as part of the reflection. This type of conference can begin with the question of what the student(s) would have given themselves if they were determining their own grade. This should be guided by the rubric that will provide some insight as to places where they believe they could have done better. If a student gives himself a lower score, that could spark a conversation as to what went wrong and what could have been done to prevent this.

You might use elements of any of the conferences in any of the other conferences. For example, you might use aspects of reflection while conducting a process conference. Or you might combine a status and process conference into one. Or you might reflect on the process and what went right or wrong. This is perfectly fine but you do need to make sure as the teacher that you are purposeful about having all of these conferences periodically with students.

Effective feedback

It isn't just enough to meet with students, they should leave the conference with some sort of actionable tasks. That is what makes the feedback effective, and according to John Hattie, this is a teaching strategy that is very valuable, placing well above typical teacher effects.

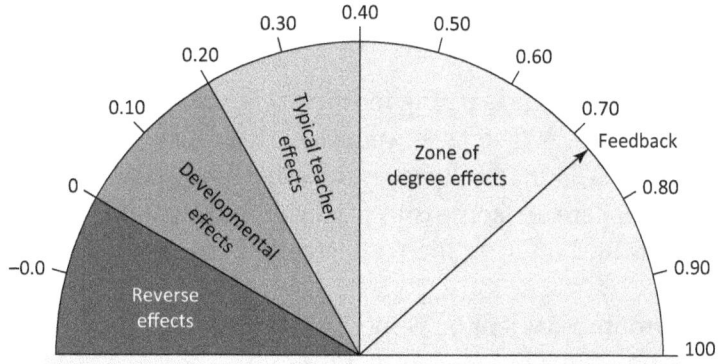

What does effective feedback look like though? There are a few things to consider when determining whether the feedback you are giving falls into that category:

- Goal referenced: feedback guides students to their goal
- Actionable: students should be able to do something with the feedback
- User-friendly: should be in language clear to the student
- Tangible and transparent: feedback should be clear

- ♦ Timely: shouldn't have to wait a while to receive it, the more immediate the better
- ♦ Ongoing: teacher is giving feedback throughout the learning process, not just at the end
- ♦ Consistent: students shouldn't hear one thing and then something contradictory the next time (Wiggins, 2012)

The feedback should be something the student can do something with. You telling a student she is doing well is encouraging and makes her feel good about herself, but it does not help her to make her work better. That would be more along the lines of, "I like what you are doing here but have you considered why they made the decision they did?" Feedback like this causes the lightbulb above the student's head to shine and she can begin to make all sorts of new connections and deepen her level of thinking.

When you are having these conversations with students and offering effective feedback, you have to be careful that you are not doing the following:

- ♦ Knowing the answer
- ♦ Dominating the conversation
- ♦ Correcting student mistakes immediately
- ♦ Being the one who decides when they move on to the next thing
- ♦ Telling them they can't do something

You need to let them do the learning for themselves which means letting them do most of the talking. As teachers, we love to fill empty classroom space with our voices. However, a master teacher does far more listening than talking. With that in mind, here are some things you should consider when conferencing with students and offering them effective feedback:

- ♦ Make sure the student does most of the talking
- ♦ Pause and affirm before commenting
- ♦ Don't interrupt
- ♦ Ask one question at a time
- ♦ Ask follow-up questions
- ♦ Avoid leading questions
- ♦ Avoid giving advice

If you are doing these things, you are giving students the space to do the learning on their own and you can sleep at night knowing that you helped them to achieve this.

The meddler in the middle

The second area where you can have an impact in the classroom without dominating it is to become what is known as the meddler in the middle. The role of the meddler is to go around the room, listening to different groups as they work on their problem, and look for opportunities to ask questions meant to meddle.

Unlike a conference where you are having a conversation with students, the meddler in the middle is more like a sniper who comes in, fires off a shot, and then quickly scurries away as the others try to reign in the chaos. Here is what it might look like:

> *Student #1:* I was reading about the trolley car dilemma.
> *Student #2:* What's that?
> *Student #1:* It is a moral philosophy simulation. You are on a trolley car heading down a track. If you continue to go straight, you kill five people. If you pull the lever and switch the track, you kill only one.
> *Student #2:* That seems easy enough, you switch the track. That way you are killing four fewer people.
> *Student #1:* But the dilemma is that you made the decision and took the action to kill that person. You are the one who had to switch the track to seal that person's fate.
> *Student #2:* That would be tougher but I would be OK knowing that I saved the lives of more people.
>   (Teacher who is walking by leans in and says to the two)
> *Teacher:* What if that one person were your mother or father?
>   (Teacher walks away, overhearing as the two continue talking)
> *Student #1:* That would be much more difficult.
> *Student #2:* But you are still harming fewer people.
> *Student #1:* Yes but you would also be emotionally harming your family and you would know you chose to kill your mom or dad.
> *Student #2:* I hadn't thought about it like that. That would be tough.

Question stems that can be used when being the meddler in the middle:

- ♦ What if…?
- ♦ Have you considered _____ perspective?
- ♦ Tell me more about…
- ♦ How might things be different if…?
- ♦ What would have to change in order for…?

- How would you justify...?
- What are you assuming that you probably shouldn't?
- How would it work if you changed...?
- What is the connection between...?
- How do you decide...?
- How does that compare to...?
- What do you suppose the motivation was?
- What question would you ask?
- What about yourself might influence your decision?
- Why is this the best solution?

By dropping these little salvos, you are blowing the minds of your students and forcing them to have to put them back together, only in a different way, which gets them thinking in a different way. This is pushing their thought process and getting them to those higher levels of thinking we want them to be at.

Cognitive task analysis

A last teaching strategy that can be used to great effect in a problem-based learning classroom is what is known as cognitive task analysis or CTA. The purpose of a CTA is to give students the awareness of the thinking skills being used by them. Because they are more aware, they are more likely to use them while trying to solve their problem. Much like you should be aware of the levels of questions you are asking in your classroom, you are trying to help students gain this level of awareness as well. Part of this is also understanding what sort of thinking they will need to use in order to answer the problem.

This involves a much more subtle form of teaching. Instead of blatantly giving students information or providing them with resources, you would be teaching CTA with every interaction you are having with students. There are four things you should be doing as you have these conversations with students:

1. Using language to encourage higher-level thinking – this means being purposeful with students about using the appropriate verbs when encouraging them to think at a higher level. Not only should you use these verbs, but students should get into the habit of using them, not just in their essential question but for any question they pose in the process of solving the problem.

    Here are some higher-level verbs you might include in your vocabulary:

Analyzing	analyze, assumption, categorize, classify, compare and contrast, conclusion, deduce, discover, dissect, distinguish, edit, examine, explain, function, infer, inspect, motive, reason, test for, validate
Evaluating	appraise, assess, award, conclude, criticize, debate, defend, determine, disprove, evaluate, give opinion, interpret, justify, judge, influence, prioritize, prove, recommend, support, verify
Creating	build, change, combine, compile, compose, construct, create, design, develop, discuss, estimate, formulate, hypothesize, imagine, integrate, invent, make up, modify, originate, organize, plan, predict, propose, rearrange, revise, suppose, theorize

2. Encouraging discussion – whenever students are working in groups on their problem, they should engage in discussions that use the language of higher-level thinking. You should be urging them to have discussions as a group, especially when making decisions that affect them all. You might want to goad them into a discussion every once in a while, starting one and then walking away and letting them take over.
3. Modeling – there will be times in a PrBL classroom where you will need to do some direct instruction, either to provide context, explaining something, or if there is a lesson that does not fit into the PrBL structure. When you are doing these, make sure you model the higher-level thinking in your questioning, directions, and activities.
4. Using images to jog memory – once students begin to understand the various levels of Bloom's Taxonomy, they may only need a friendly reminder to take it to the next level. This can be something as simple as an image (Wichtowska).

   For example, let's say you are walking around the room and you see a student intently working but you notice he could take it a step further. You could jot down on a sticky note something like this:

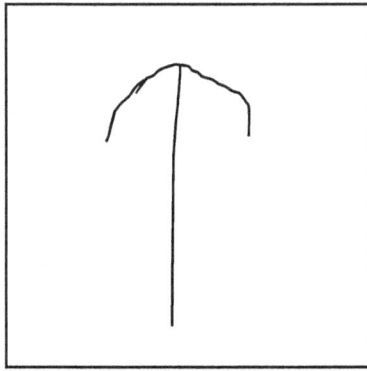

This gives students a signal that they need to take it to the next level without interrupting their work process. Or you might lean down and jot on their paper:

A more formal image system to use would be the Depth and Complexity icons developed by Kaplan and Taylor. These are 11 icons that can be used to get students to think about their work in a different way. For example, if you were to use this icon on their work...

...this would trigger students to consider other perspectives on the problem that might lead to certain insights. Or if this icon was used...

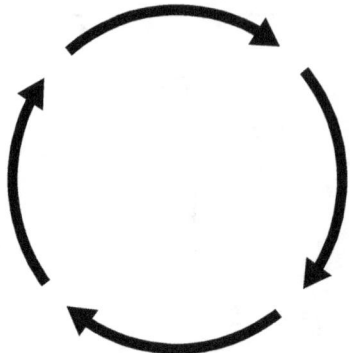

...students would be prompted to look at how their problem might change over time. Would the solution be the same ten years from now, 50 years from now, 100? This would give students something interesting to consider.

If you would like further information on the Depth and Complexity icons, you can watch this video tutorial https://www.youtube.com/watch?v=R-zxPbR1RXw.

https://neap.com.au/how-students-awareness-of-thinking-improves-grades/

The CTA is the HOW of creating the culture in your classroom for students to engage in higher-level thinking, the sort of thinking you want your gifted students to be doing.

Do we have a problem here?

The role of the teacher shifts mightily in a problem-based learning classroom. Instead of being the sage from the stage, you are now the guide from the side. And you should take that guide moniker seriously, making sure that the students are doing most of the work and you are there to help them along the way should they need it, pointing them in the right direction only when absolutely necessary. When you are doing this you want to maintain the guide role and not the sage, getting them to think at a higher level. Some things to remember while giving feedback or suggestions to students:

- Should be open-ended so that students are not limited to a correct response
- Make neutral statements or questions as much as possible, do not take sides in the discussion
- Pose "what if" scenarios for students to ponder
- Make controversial comments that will force students to take a side and form an opinion
- If the class seems to overwhelmingly be leaning toward a side, be the devil's advocate and bring up things you may not agree with but that will spark discussion

The benefit of such a role is that you get to have conversations, and while meeting with students, personalizing the learning. Students also learn how to learn for themselves, which will benefit them beyond your classroom walls.

Activity #9

How do you make your teaching more authentic? Consider these six methods for making your classroom one in which you are a more authentic teacher (taken from the book Authentic Learning: Real-World Experiences that Build 21st Century Skills*).*

- *Staying away from the front of the classroom*
- *Avoiding just giving information*
- *Not doing more work than the students*
- *Not being the sole source of evaluation*
- *Allowing for productive struggle*
- *Trusting your students (Stanley, 2018)*

Reflect upon each of these and your own practices. Are there some of these that you aren't doing and how could you begin to incorporate them into your role as the teacher. Are there others you could do a better job of and what would that look like?

Conclusion

Houston, We Have a Problem

If you need proof of the power of problem-based learning, look no further than the US space program. There are many examples of times where NASA was faced with a problem, a problem with no precedence, and somehow had to figure out a solution WITHOUT KILLING ANYONE. This problem came to a head in 1962 when John F. Kennedy, addressing a group of 40,000 people in Rice Stadium in Texas, threw down the gauntlet in the space race and claimed the United States would land a man on the moon and return him safely to Earth. We didn't know how to do this, what this would entail, or more importantly, what awaited us once we got to the moon. And yet by 1969, a mere seven years later, Neil Armstrong made his historic descent down the ladder and said those famous words of how this was one small step for man, one giant leap for mankind, becoming the first man on the moon.

Of course, often all we remember is the happy ending. Prior to this are all of the things that had to come before this great accomplishment could be achieved. The most eye-opening of these is all of the failures. Failure when astronauts were subjected to a device where they are spun in all sorts of directions and have to make it stable before passing out, often throwing up at the end (that would not be good in a space helmet). The tragedy of the crew of Apollo 1 dying in a fire was certainly not a success. There was the time Armstrong was testing the Lunar Landing Research Vehicle and had to eject moments before it would have killed him. It seems like there are far more failures than there are successes, but then that's the point of it all, isn't it?

Like Armstrong himself said, "We need to fail. We need to fail down here so we don't fail up there." A failure up there results in lives being lost. A failure down here is a learning opportunity. This is the ultimate lesson of problem-based learning; it is not always about the successes; it is the journey we take while getting there.

That is the beauty of problem solving. You get to make lots of attempts until you succeed. This goes for a scientist who is trying all sorts of different combinations until he comes upon the one that will make his experiment a success, to the kid playing video games who gets stuck on a challenging level, trying and failing over and over and over until finally advancing to the next level. The space program in general was all about problem solving. The movie *Hidden Figures* showed us the people behind the scenes who had to mathematically figure out how to get John Glenn into orbit and back down. They actually had to invent math in order to make this possible. All three of the protagonists had to problem solve in order to succeed. Mary identifies a flaw in the heat shield. Dorothy sees that she and her team are going to soon be replaced by computers so she learns to program them to make herself relevant. Katherine figures out the final landing coordinates that will enable NASA to find where Glenn is landing. Without these problems being solved, things might have turned out very differently.

Another example would be Apollo 13, the ultimate failed mission where the astronauts and folks at NASA had to figure out how to bring a defective spacecraft back to Earth without killing the crew on board. At one point they discovered that the carbon dioxide level was becoming high and they had to figure out a way to adapt a filter to a pump, literally having to make a square peg fit into a round hole, using only the equipment on board. This problem solving continued when the people on the ground had to figure out how to power up the module without using too much energy that would be needed to get them home. Ken Mattingly went through the sequence many times, failing with each attempt, before finally landing on the successful sequence. Without that process, those astronauts don't come home.

This sort of authentic problem solving is powerful because people are not just solving random problems that once shared, will simply be pitched or discarded. These are authentic solutions that solve a real problem and advance our understanding. We need to do more of this in the classroom. We need to be putting students in authentic situations and having them develop a solution that will have an impact on their world.

The most amazing thing about the space program is that in most cases, the folks didn't know what they were doing. No one had ever been to space before. No one had walked on the moon. How do you problem solve for something you are not even sure you know the answer to? That is the challenge in preparing our students for the real world. We no longer know what jobs/careers are going to be available for them once they enter the workforce. How do we prepare them for jobs that don't exist? We teach them how to problem solve anything, and they can apply it to whatever situation they find themselves in.

This problem solving in space has continued even to current times. Currently, Elon Musk is trying to figure out how we can send people to Mars. He even has the problem solving all mapped out in his presentation that can be found here: www.spacex.com/sites/spacex/files/making_life_multiplanetary -2017.pdf. Jeff Bezos and Richard Branson are trying to reinvent the way we travel to space by developing a ship that space tourists can use.

NASA recently sent out an edict that they would award $35,000 to anyone who could make a better toilet for their astronauts. They called it the Lunar Loo challenge and the reason for it was that NASA scientists and engineers, with all of their infinite wisdom, had not really had a good system before. Some of the methods used back when we were regularly taking trips to the moon involved astronauts peeing into a roll-on cuff, pooping into bags, or wearing space diapers. With the advent of the Artemis Project, vowing to put a person on the moon by 2024 for the first time since 1972, they asked for the public's help with designing a better toilet. Certain constraints had to be followed. The toilet must:

- Function in both microgravity and lunar gravity
- Have a mass of less than 15 kg in Earth's gravity
- Occupy a volume no greater than 0.12 m^3
- Consume less than 70 Watts of power
- Operate with a noise level under 60 decibels (no louder than an average bathroom fan)
- Accommodate both female and male users
- Accommodate users ranging from 58 to 77 inches tall and 107 to 290 lbs in weight

There were over 2000 entries in this problem-solving contest as well as a junior division where another nearly 1000 entries came from people 18 years of age and below. The winning design was the following:

THRONE (Translunar Hypercritical Repository 1) involved the innovative idea of a bladeless fan to entrain waste as a good alternative idea compared with the typical suction/vacuum pump system. The team also came up with a system to minimize crew interaction with waste bags, using a diaper genie-type concept to keep the waste bagged, facilitating easy turnaround between uses.

The reason the space program is such a good example of problem-based learning is that it actually had to work. They didn't want an astronaut to get into space only to discover there was a problem that had not been considered. All of the problem solving had to take place before an astronaut even broke through the atmosphere.

Appendix A

A PrBL for You

This book has suggested that when you design a problem-based learning lesson, you need to turn over a lot of the work to the students. That is actually the largest benefit of PrBL (not that you don't have to do so much work, although that is a nice perk) – that students are given autonomy over what they are learning, how they are learning it, and in which direction the learning will go. In order to have that benefit, you as the teacher have to walk a fine line. You have to give students enough material to get started on the lesson, but not so much that you are leading them along.

This book has hopefully given you lots of guidance on how you could structure your PrBL classroom, but it hasn't given you the lessons themselves. That is up to you the teacher. This book very easily could have taken the approach of providing you with problem-based learning lessons that you could follow much like a substitute teacher executes the lesson plans you leave for them. However, that does not personalize the lesson for your particular classroom.

With that in mind, this section will provide you with a complete problem-based learning lesson that would be relevant to you as a teacher – creating a problem-based learning assignment that would be relevant to your students. It will go step by step through the PrBL process and give an example of what it might look like for you as a teacher.

Step 1 – Present the problem

As was discussed in Chapter 6, a good problem is one that is ill-defined. Here is an example of a problem that is ill-defined:

Create a lesson for your class that uses the problem-based learning process.

This is ill-defined because we don't know what the lesson is, who the class is, and what shape this PrBL will take. Some of these will be resolved in step 2.

Step 2 – List what is known

Just the facts ma'am. When you are listing what is known, you are not speculating or trying to predict a possible outcome. You are simply listing facts that might better define aspects of your ill-defined problem. Here is an example a teacher might come up with:

- Grade 6 students
- Have done one PrBL lesson previously so will need more guidance in decisions
- Social studies
- Economics
- Already understand the basic concepts of economics such as supply and demand, scarcity, and surplus
- Will have to learn about marketing and writing a business plan
- Would like them to work in groups
- Have three weeks for the lesson
- Need to have an authentic assessment with an authentic audience

Step 3 – Develop a problem statement

Once all of the facts are considered, you have to develop a problem statement that potentially solves the problem. You might use a graphic organizer such as this in order to arrange your thoughts:

Topic:

Essential question:

Duration of lesson:

Learning outcomes:

- ♦
- ♦
- ♦

Goal(s):

Authentic product:

Authentic audience:

You would simply fill in as many of these as possible, which would help you to determine the problem statement. For this particular lesson it could look like this:

Topic: Economics (marketing)

Essential question: How does one successfully market a product that makes people want to buy it?

Duration of lesson: Three weeks

Learning outcomes:
- ♦ Students will understand how to and then create their own business plan.
- ♦ Students will understand how the economic terms work together to create a need in the market that can be filled with specific products.
- ♦ Students will determine how to effectively market their product through the creation of a commercial.
- ♦ Students will learn the qualities of a successful pitch and then attempt to make their own.

Goal(s): Students will develop the confidence to be able to make a professional pitch to a group of professionals while at the same time learning the economic concepts required for the lesson.

Authentic product: Students will have to:
1) Create a product that can be marketed
2) Write a business plan that shows how this will be done
3) Create a commercial that can be shown
4) Give a five-minute pitch to present their business plan

Authentic audience: Ask local businesspeople to come in and serve as a panel that students present to.

In this case, the teacher has to teach his sixth graders how to market a product as well as create a business plan. A problem statement might look like this:

> Students will show what they learned about marketing by pitching a product complete with a commercial and business plan.

Step 4 – List what is needed/ask questions

Then you create your to-do list in order to accomplish solving the problem. The list is all the things you need to provide or have answered in order to move forward with the lesson. Some of this might be answered by the decisions that were made in step 3.

- Understanding a business plan
- Understanding effective commercials
- Understanding successful persuasive public speaking
- What does a business plan look like?
- What makes a good commercial?
- What will the final product look like?
- What makes for persuasive public speaking?
- How will product determine mastery?
- How will it be graded?
- Who will act as the authentic audience?
- How do you evaluate students' individual work in a group?

Step 5 – List actions, solutions, or hypothesis

You take the questions from step 4 and answer them to determine what actions and solutions you must come up with. You might even use a calendar to plot out what this will look like:

Introduce problem	Develop product	Develop product	What is a business plan?	Work on business plan
Work on business plan	Work on business plan	What makes a commercial effective?	Write/plan commercial	Film commercial
What makes for persuasive public speaking?	Plan the pitch	Plan the pitch	Practice the pitch	Presentation of business plan

This provides you with a pretty clear understanding of how the lesson will play out. There might be changes made here or there. You might choose to do lessons for the skills needed or you might task students with finding their own examples and determining how they can use them. Students might not need two days to plan the pitch so this merely gives them more time to practice and refine.

Step 6 – Present and support the solution

Now that you have made all of the decisions, you have to figure out how to communicate this with others, in this case, your students. This is your product. It could be in the form of syllabi or a rubric so that expectations are clear. A final product that demonstrates your solution might look like this:

> **SHARK TANK**
>
> Students will participate in a Shark Tank where they must pitch an idea for a product of their own creation. Part of this is creating a business plan that explains the economic principles behind it and having a commercial that markets the features of the product.
>
> **Objective**. The goal of this lesson is to design a start-up business that you will be presenting to a group of investors for start-up money. You are to create your own product or service, but you must market to the investors why they should invest in you; why is your product or service better than what is already out there? Or is there nothing else like it and you are creating your own market?
>
> The work teams will consist of **three to a group**. You will be given some time in class to work. Each of you will be responsible for specific roles. Below you will see the descriptions. Before you start, you must tell me who is taking on what role.
>
> - ★ **Manager – Your specific role is to make sure your group is on a specific task every day**. You must create a deadline for everything that needs to be done. This means that you have to make sure your team is doing what they are supposed to be doing. For each time you meet, you are to record what you are working on during the time given to you. Time management is crucial.
> - ★ **Tech – Your specific role is to design and edit the presentation that you will be giving to the investors**. You must make sure that the final product is working and ready to go the day *before* it is due.
> - ★ **Reporter/writer** – Your specific role is to make sure the business plan is put together in the right order, including a title page and page numbers. Although everyone will be writing specific sections, **you are responsible for making sure that the final draft is free from grammar errors, and that it makes sense.**

Part 1 – About your business. Before you start this writing part of this project, you must brainstorm about a business and product that you want to start and create. Your first task is to decide on a product or service. You will conduct a **brief presentation (< 5 minutes)** telling the rest of the class **what you are doing and why. You must include the name of the business, who is taking on what role, the type of business you are setting up, and what product and/or services will you be offering**. This is to be professional and **everyone in the group must speak**.

Part 2 – Writing the business plan. You will be writing a business plan that outlines your new start-up company. **The best way to write a business plan is to do one section at a time**.

Part 3 – Commercial. Create a commercial clip of your business service and/or product. The commercial should include at least a slogan, music, service, or product in action, as well as showing **creativity**.

Part 4 – Presenting to the sharks. You will present your proposal to the investors. Don't forget to include how much money you would like for what percentage of ownership, and what you plan to do with the investors' money. Keep in mind that you are fighting everyone else in the class for the start-up money (only one group will win), so you have to get creative with your presentation. You may present using PowerPoint, posters, short video clips, Prezi, handouts, demonstration, and so on. Remember this should be creative! Dressing up is a must! **You must also create a physical model of your product that you can show during your presentation**. Points given will be based on creativity and effort.

After the presentation, the investors will have a chance to ask questions about your business, your target market, your financials, or any other aspect that needs to be analyzed in order for them to make a decision.

After all the presentations are done, a winner will be selected.

Grading (500 points possible): you will be graded on the following:
Part I
Introductory presentation (50 points)
Commercial (50 points)
Presentation/sales pitch (200 points)
Part II
Business plan (200 points)

This then needs to be presented to students so that they are clear on the expectations. Notice there are plenty of places for students to make choices as it is not clearly defined what a business plan is, what goes into a commercial, or what product they will create. Students have a good amount of autonomy to make these decisions, which connects them to the learning more.

Appendix B

The Matrix

Various suggestions for how to use the matrix:

- Read through these choices and choose ones that would be appropriate or applicable to your PrBL from each of the four matrixes.
- Choose selections from each of the categories.
- Give students the matrixes and have them select.
- Put the numbers 1 through to 24 into a bag or find a 24-sided die.
- Close your eyes and point to a box in the matrix selector four times.
- Take four coins and throw them into the air and see where they land on the matrix selector.
- Use the corresponding number across all matrixes (i.e., 1, 1, 1, 1).

Problems:

School	City/state	National	World
1. Students need to be nicer to each other	2. The local river has become polluted	3. There are too many animals without homes	4. We waste a lot of water
5. The cafeteria needs healthier choices	6. People need help during the holidays	7. The elderly need to feel useful	8. A lot of animals are killed for personal wealth
9. Sports seem to be more important than academics	10. The library needs to get more kids into their location	11. Lots of kids are obese	12. Education is not accessible to all
13. There are too many students in a classroom	14. There are some unfair laws in our city/state	15. Should there be gun control?	16. Some governments do bad things for their people
17. The playground is boring	18. We need a way to allow our fire and police to respond faster	19. Is social media a good or bad thing?	20. Should countries still be stockpiling nuclear weapons?
21. Parents put too much pressure on students	22. What does the budget for education look like in our city/state?	23. Should there be universal medical insurance in the US?	24. Why should/should not countries limit the number of immigrants?

Product:

Audio	Visual	Verbal	Performance
1. Podcast	2. Art	3. Vlog	4. Journal
5. Interview	6. Model	7. TED Talk	8. Email
9. Song	10. Exhibition	11. Lesson	12. Webpage
13. Play	14. PPT/Google Slides	15. Presentation/demonstration	16. Short Story
17. Poem	18. Poster/chart	19. Debate/oral defense	20. Brochure
21. Film	22. Storyboard	23. Role playing/ skit	24. Essay

Audience:

School community	City community	Experts	Universities
1. Other classes of students	2. City council	3. Professionals in the field	4. University professors
5. Other teachers	6. Chamber of commerce	7. Writer's groups	8. Graduate students
9. Older students	10. Parks department	11. Professional organizations	12. Students within a particular major
13. Administration	14. Library	15. Mentors	16. Alumni
17. School Board	18. Local businesses	19. Hobbyists	20. Admissions officers

Technology options to make sharing of PrBL products authentic:

1. YouTube	2. Kahoot	3. Pecha Kucha	4. Sketchnote
5. Chat boards	6. Slideshare	7. Binge watch	8. Google Doodle
9. Amazon reviews	10. Website	11. App	12. Infographic
13. Online publishing	14. Anchor podcast	15. Brick builder	16. Create a memorial
17. Zoom/Google Meet	18. Playback	19. Stop motion	20. Poster session

Matrix selector

1	7	13	19
2	8	14	20
3	9	15	21
4	10	16	22
5	11	17	23
6	12	18	24

Works Cited

Atkins, S., and Murphy, K. (1994). Reflective Practice. *Nursing Standard*, *8*(39), 49–56.

Boud, D., Keogh, R., and Walker, D. (1994). *Reflection: Turning Experience into Learning.* London: Kogan Page.

Duch, B.J., Groh, S.E., and Allen, D.E. (2001). Why Problem-Based Learning? A Case Study of Institutional Change in Undergraduate Education. In B. Duch, S. Groh, and D. Allen (Eds.), *The Power of Problem-Based Learning* (pp. 3–11). Sterling, VA: Stylus.

Fairbanks, B. (2021). 8 Professional Soft Skills You Need for the Workplace and How to Get Them. University of Phoenix. August 18, 2021. Retrieved from https://www.phoenix.edu/blog/8-professional-soft-skills-you-need-for-the-workplace-and-how-to-get-them.html

Francis, E.M. (2016). *Now THAT'S a Good Question! How to Promote Cognitive Rigor Through Classroom Questioning.* Alexandria, VA: ASCD.

Francis, E.M. (2021). *Deconstructing Depth of Knowledge: A Method and Model for Deeper Teaching and Learning.* Bloomington, IN: Solution Tree.

Global Fitness for Work: Employer Perspective. Global People. (n.d.) Retrieved from https://warwick.ac.uk/fac/cross_fac/globalpeople2/companies/employersurveys/

Gibbs, G. (1988). *Learning by Doing: A Guide to Teaching and Learning Methods.* Oxford: Oxford Polytechnic.

Jones, R.D. (2004). *Introduction to Rigor/Relevance Framework.* Rexford, NY: International Center for Leadership in Education.

Kember, D., McKay, J., Sinclair, K., and Wong, F.K.Y. (2008). A Four-Category Scheme for Coding and Assessing the Level of Reflection in Written Work. *Assessment & Evaluation in Higher Education*, *33*(4), 363–379.

Marr, B. (2019). The 10+ Most Important Job Skills Every Company Will Be Looking For In 2020. Forbes. October 28, 2019. Retrieved from https://www.forbes.com/sites/bernardmarr/2019/10/28/the-10-most-important-job-skills-every-company-will-be-looking-for-in-2020/?sh=4bfca5ed67b6

The Motivation Puzzle: Four Ways to Helps Students Succeed. (2016). September 8, 2016. Apex Learning. Retrieved from https://www.apexlearning.com/blog/the-motivation-puzzle-four-ways-to-help-students-succeed

Reeves, T.C., Herrington, J., and Oliver, R. (2002). Authentic Activity as a Model for Web-Based Learning. 2002 Annual Meeting of the American Educational Research Association, New Orleans, LA, USA.

Sloane, D. What are Some Strategies for Reflection Activities? UMSL Center for Teaching and Learning. Retrieved from http://www.umsl.edu/services/ctl/faculty/instructionalsupport/reflection-strat.html

Stanley, T. (2014). *Performance-Based Assessment for 21st Century Skills*. Waco, TX: Prufrock Press.

Stanley, T. (2018). *Authentic Learning: Real-World Experiences that Build 21st Century Skills*. Waco, TX: Prufrock Press.

Wagner, T. (2008). *The Global Achievement Gap: Why Even Our Best Schools Don't Teach the New Survival Skills Our Children Need – And What We Can Do About It*. New York: Basic Books.

Wichtowska, S. How Students' Awareness of Thinking Improves Grades. NEAP. Retrieved from https://neap.com.au/how-students-awareness-of-thinking-improves-grades/

Wiggins, G. (2007). What is an Essential Question? Big Ideas: An Authentic Education e-Journal. November 15, 2007. Retrieved from https://www.authenticeducation.org/ae_bigideas/article.lasso?artid=53

World Economic Forum. (2020). The Future of Jobs Report 2020. October 2020. Retrieved from https://www3.weforum.org/docs/WEF_Future_of_Jobs_2020.pdf

Wiggins, G. (2012). Seven keys to effective feedback. *ASCD Educational Leadership,* 70(1), 10–16.

For Product Safety Concerns and Information please contact our EU
representative GPSR@taylorandfrancis.com
Taylor & Francis Verlag GmbH, Kaufingerstraße 24, 80331 München, Germany

www.ingramcontent.com/pod-product-compliance
Lightning Source LLC
Chambersburg PA
CBHW080939300426
44115CB00017B/2886